PRAISE FOR BULLETPROOF SELLING

Bulletproof Selling is packed full of powerful tactics that you can immediately apply to your sales processes. If you follow Shawn's advice, I can guarantee your cash flow and confidence will skyrocket.

– Lt. Col. USAF (ret.) Waldo Waldman, author of the New York Times and Wall Street Journal Bestseller *Never Fly Solo* and member of the Speaker's Hall of Fame

Warning, do not read the book without a highlighter and notepad! This is not another sales book; it is a power tool. Some books talk about sales, but this book shows step-by-step what it takes to make sales success happen.

– Mark Hunter, "The Sales Hunter," best-selling author of *A Mind For Sales*

As someone who has seen firsthand how our service men and women constantly adapt to ever-changing environments, I can attest that to become better, the understanding and use of different systems and modalities are critical to success. Shawn has done the work of bridging those time tested and proven systems we used in combat to the systems salespeople need to be successful on the battlefield of business.

– Dr. Aaron Tucker, CEO of AT Solutions and former Navy SEAL

Shawn has created something in this book that every salesperson needs – a bridge between knowing what to do and actually doing it when selling. This is a complete guide for turning a sales team into a sales force.

– Commander Mary C. Kelly, USN (retired), and member of the Speaker's Hall of Fame

What you know is not the key, it's what you DO that scores wins. Shawn Rhodes shows you how to make unshakable work habits out of your ideas. Habits are your armor against distraction and weakness. USE this book!!!

– Jim Cathcart, Member of The Sales & Marketing Hall of Fame and author of *Relationship Selling*

Bulletproof Selling cracks the code and solves the challenge of how to be consistent, efficient, scale, and be more productive. Instead of telling you what to do, Shawn lays out step-by-step how to do it. This book is a go-to-guide to take your sales and your business to the next level.

– Meridith Elliott Powell, business strategist, award-winning author and CEO of Motionfirst

Whether a business is publicly traded or family-run, it has to be great at selling if it wants to survive. In *Bulletproof Selling*, Shawn Rhodes has created something any business owner or salesperson can use to capture what works so their business can survive today and thrive tomorrow. Get your pen and notebook ready when you sit down with this powerful book! I recommend this book without reservation.

– Barry Banther, CEO of Banther Consulting, best-selling author, and member of the Speaker's Hall of Fame

The best salespeople actively change their behavior to unexpected obstacles and opportunities. Shawn's system, borrowed from the best militaries in the world, ensures salespeople repeat what works and continue to adapt when environments change.

– Dr. Yuval Lirov, CEO of Vericle, Inc.

BULLETPROOF SELLING:

SYSTEMIZING SALES
for the
BATTLEFIELD OF BUSINESS

SHAWN RHODES

Edited by Serena Fisher

Dedication

To Elyse, the greatest sale of my life and the one I get to re-make every day.

Also By Shawn Rhodes:

Pivot Point: Turn On A Dime Without Sacrificing Results

Universal Export: A Guide For Overachievers in Working Less And Enjoying More

CONTENTS

SECTION III
Becoming Bulletproof

FORWARD

The ability to acquire and retain customers is the lifeblood of every organization. The harsh reality is the business you are looking to win is either already in the hands of someone else, or you have dozens of other people fighting for the exact same dollars.

After training more than 2 million people around the world, my hope is that those people have learned *Exactly What To Say*, *Exactly How To Sell*, and *Exactly Where To Start* in order to grow their sales and businesses.

Without true discipline, practical application, and accountability, the lessons learned in any training session sadly become reduced to anecdotes, quotes on social media, and fail to reap the rewards people knew were really possible.

Success requires people on the front lines of business – salespeople – to apply what they've learned in trainings, follow through on their responsibilities and then repeat again, day after day after day.

Whilst it's the goal of every speaker, trainer, and coach to make a lasting impact on their audiences, we can't do the work for them.

In sports, in business and on the battlefield, it is those that commit fully to their training and then use that training in reality that achieve greatness.

Unfortunately, there's only so much any salesperson can recall from memory. When faced with the stress of making another prospecting call, negotiating with a potential client, or balancing personal and professional challenges, our ability to remember what we picked up from the last book we read or workshop we attended disappears. The problem is rarely a lack of great sales processes, it's that those processes are rarely turned into repeatable *systems*.

It's at this point many people turn to "hope" as their strategy. It's too easy to believe that charm, experience, and rapid memory recall will serve you in the moments that matter.

Shawn Rhodes comes from a world where "hoping" for success was unacceptable and excellence was the expected minimum standard. Through his multiple combat tours in the U.S. Marines studying how the highest performers applied systems to achieve success, he's been able to translate that experience to help salespeople reach the same standards of discipline, precision, and performance. Thousands of people have now been able to replace hope with certainty through proven systems that create predictable outcomes and deliver the accountability that holds so many people back.

Throughout this book, Shawn walks salespeople and sales leaders through the steps required to systemize their own selling processes, from pipeline creation to standing up omni-channel campaigns to sales meetings to referral generation. This not only makes the book a valuable primer for those standing up a sales organization from scratch, but also assists senior salespeople in refining the lessons they've learned over a career. Shawn has aided thousands of business leaders and salespeople in pivoting their sales and operations. In this book, he applies what he's learned so any business can benefit from systemizing their sales, whether they're a team of thousands or a team of one.

This book deserves a place on the shelf of everyone who is committed to sales success, not because it is full of new ideas and sales hacks to fast track results. Instead, it's because it helps sales professionals to systemize their wisdom and experience to create consistent high performance.

This won't tell you *EXACTLY what to say*, but it will ensure you use *EXACTLY what you've spent a lifetime learning.*

Phil M Jones,
Best Selling Author – *Exactly What to Say*

PREFACE

Hope is not a sales strategy.

WITHOUT KNOWING YOU or your company, whether you have decades of experience or are brand new to sales, whether you are an entrepreneur or whether you manage hundreds of salespeople, I know you are using hope more than you should. You're likely...

Hoping you remember how to overcome objections.

Hoping that awesome tip you got from a sales trainer or book comes to mind the next time you pick up the phone.

Hoping your next prospect has budget, need, and authority to buy what you or your salespeople are selling.

Does this mean the books, courses, seminars, and sales trainers you've invested in aren't doing their jobs? Absolutely not. There are hundreds of awesome books and programs by great sales trainers that provide great strategies and tactics to improve sales.

The problem isn't the content you've been consuming. It isn't the trainers' effectiveness. The reason I know hope is playing a larger part than it should in your sales strategy is that – despite all of your investments in development and education – you and your salespeople are still *hoping* you'll remember all you've learned and experienced when in front of the next prospect.

Sales teams around the world are *hoping* the objection turnarounds, email scripts, call flows, and negotiation tactics they've invested time and money in learning are actually used.

3

Salespeople are *hoping* they remember to add new leads each week to their pipelines, get all their outreach accomplished, update the CRM (Customer Relationship Management tool), and meet sales goals, while *hoping* to spend time with their families.

You're not alone if you find yourself relying on hope more than you should. Most salespeople, regardless of their industry, experience, or resources, are using hope as the foundation of their sales strategy. They pour money into sales training, books, and seminars and then wonder why they, and their teams, don't get consistently better results. The training you and your company are investing in isn't broken. Rather, it's that the sales training we're receiving is designed for a predictable environment and for salespeople that hopefully remember everything they've learned.

As any veteran salesperson can attest, sales is a battlefield. It's stressful, taxing, and there are unknown pitfalls around every corner. Salespeople are cut down on this battlefield every single day not because they don't know how to sell, but because their hope fails them.

The purpose of this book is not to give you a magic formula that will solve your prospecting, selling, negotiating, closing, and referral-generation challenges – although we'll address each of those areas. I could never recreate the brilliant work of the sales masters that came before me. What I can do is help ensure you consistently *use* what you and your teams learn, show you how to innovate those types of solutions for yourselves and how to guarantee those systems are consistently used across your prospects.

What would change if you and your salespeople knew what was working as of <u>this moment</u> in prospecting, selling, closing deals, and generating referrals in your industry?

What would happen if every lost sale was something your entire team learned from? And you could ensure no one lost a deal for that reason again?

PREFACE

How many new sales would it generate if your team was measurably better every week at prospecting, eliciting interest, and winning clients from your competitors?

How it would feel to have your salespeople actively capturing successes and challenges throughout their week and willingly sharing those lessons with teammates?

What would change in your results if your team had access to every lesson your salespeople had learned through the course of their careers and could access them from anywhere in the world?

What could you achieve if instead of *hoping* the great tips you picked up in that last sales book or training program were used, you *knew* they were being utilized with every prospect, in every negotiation, and with every client?

This book represents the first time a systemized way of selling has been made available to anyone outside our own consulting clients. By using what we share here, hope will no longer have a part in your sales strategy.

This isn't another book focused simply on sales tactics or leveraging the latest social media strategy. Instead, this is a book on how to optimize the performance of *any* sales tactic or strategy. It's a book about replacing the hope you were relying on with *certainty*. Maybe you're managing a veteran sales team. Perhaps you're a salesperson interested in being better than you were yesterday. You might even be an entrepreneur who would rejoice with any uptick in revenue. Utilizing what's in these pages will provide the certainty salespeople strive entire careers to achieve.

Instead of another book on 'sales tips,' this book will explain how to see *selling* in a new way: the creation of manageable, scalable systems to capture what's working in your sales activities and eliminate what's not. We'll show you how to forge, assemble, and start a systems-based sales engine that adapts to the changes salespeople face.

No matter what the economy does, regardless of how many salespeople retire or jump ship, whether the effects of a global pandemic are still affecting your industry, this book will show you how to leverage change to serve your sales goals and your clients' success. As your competitors' revenues are ripped apart by the impact of a virus or changing customer needs, you'll watch those challenges bounce harmlessly off of you and your team as you adapt faster than the changes occur.

After all, the world doesn't need another sales book. What it desperately needs is a way to ensure all the tips you and your team have learned from sales books, programs, and sales trainers are actually used!

It's time to put everything we've learned about selling to work in our pipelines, outreach, sales calls, and meetings.

It's time to build new strategies and systems to help us improvise solutions and make selling something that doesn't rely on hope.

It's time to make selling Bulletproof.

INTRODUCTION: BECOMING BULLETPROOF

WHEN PEOPLE THINK of being 'Bulletproof,' they usually think of superheroes and write the idea off as fantasy. But there are folks like you and I, folks with families and mortgages, who actually *are* Bulletproof, and they've revolutionized the way a whole generation of salespeople are selling.

2004 – Iraq

When most teenagers were entering the workforce or sitting in a university classroom, I was halfway around the world in the middle of a warzone. My job as a US Marine, in addition to being a rifleman, was to find men and women doing extraordinary things, innovating solutions that would save countless lives. It was in the city of Fallujah, during Operation Phantom Fury, that I met my first team of Bulletproof people.

At first glance, nothing about this team indicated special powers. Because of their identical uniforms, gear, and haircuts, they were almost indistinguishable from the thousands of other US Marines tasked with liberating the city. These Marines were from average hometowns across America, and none of them arrived from an alien planet or suffered an experiment gone wrong that gave them bullet-dodging powers.

Despite their uniform appearance, they *did* possess superpowers. They were each the recipients of hundreds of thousands of dollars' worth of training culled from more than 200 years of trial and error. It wasn't until I saw these superpowers in action that I understood how it improved their performance on the battlefield – and later began to realize what they could teach to every salesperson on the planet.

April 22, 2004 – Inside Fallujah

The infantry battalion I'd been attached to was tasked with operating in the Sunni Triangle of Iraq – the geography marked between Baghdad, Ramadi, and Fallujah. In April of 2004, they were deployed into Fallujah to support the largest urban assault the US military had ever conducted. As the Marines went house-to-house securing the city, I was accompanying a group of scout-snipers. That was the first team who showed me it was possible to be Bulletproof.

When the four-man team approached their first house, they walked in a spread-out column. Once their team leader identified the next building they'd been tasked to clear, he silently signaled towards the front door. The team shifted from being four separate individuals to become a single entity. I watched them stack outside the front door of the building, making sure to not stand directly in the doorway in case someone inside began shooting through it. As they entered the building, I saw what being Bulletproof was all about.

This team had never been in those buildings before. They had no idea what rooms branched off which or where stairwells would be. However, watching them move from the first room and into the second, it appeared as if they'd trained in this exact building for months. When they moved through the house, the team shifted without words or even nonverbal signals as they covered all the possible angles of attack with their rifles. Moving from room to room, they shifted fluidly as they scanned for threats like a motion-sensing machine.

That fluid movement through an unfamiliar environment wasn't a one-time fluke. If they were ordered to exit the house and re-clear it, their steps and route would have been almost identical. The same team members in the same places in line, rifles shifting in the same way as they moved from one room to the next. They were able to stay alive in this environment not because they had superhuman powers, but because their superhuman performance had been *systemized*.

Why did the US military spend so much time training their people to act as a singular entity in these situations? How had this team – and all the rest of the service members I studied – learned to be *Bulletproof?*

At its simplest, the answer is that those Marines were Bulletproof because of all the times their predecessors *hadn't been*. These Marines learned to move around corners in a certain way because of the time someone didn't and hadn't made it home. Because their lessons were hard learned, their predecessors transferred every mistake and lucky break they could into systems that would make the next generation of warfighters more successful.

The US military was focused on making people Bulletproof on the battlefield. More than a decade later, I saw that same process could be applied to making *salespeople* Bulletproof as well.

Present Day – Studying Salespeople

These days, I continue to study the best performers in the world. Instead of doing that in combat, I work to improve the performance of business and sales teams. Like the troops I served with, salespeople come from hometowns across America, from rich and poor homes, and from every ethnicity. The exceptional ones are in high demand for one reason – they sell more. Unfortunately, the more successful salespeople are, the more they become a hindrance to the overall success of their teams and companies. Why? Most salespeople are far from Bulletproof. They tend to rely upon hope, meaning if they don't remember what worked or didn't work with a past prospect, they can't reliably execute when those challenges appear in the next conversation or sale.

This results in the performance hurdles that sales managers struggle with:

- Spin-up time of salespeople and the cost of training new ones
- High turnover and the need to constantly search for more salespeople to be 'on deck'
- Dragging veteran salespeople kicking and screaming into the future of technology and using CRMs
- Cutting margins to the bone as more competitors enter the market, reducing profits and commissions
- Getting salespeople to communicate a consistent message to prospects
- Difficulty in transferring one salesperson's mistakes to lessons that benefit the entire team
- Being hamstrung in growth by a few high performers who aren't team players but produce too much revenue to be replaced

To address those issues, this book is divided into three sections, depending on where a reader is in their sales journey. While each is essential in standing up, operating, and improving a comprehensive Bulletproof selling system, each salesperson or sales leader is coming to this book with a different set of experiences and a varying degree of systems already in place.

In *Section I: Systemizing Sales*, you will find an outline describing how to construct a pipeline, as well as how to define the deal stages that make up that pipeline. Next, you'll learn how to construct omni-channel campaign systems for each of those deal stages. This section will be essential for any salesperson standing up or revamping their sales systems and will be a refresher for those salespeople already managing pipelines and campaign-driven outreach.

Section II: Sales Systems will address a variety of systems which are essential for success when prospect-facing. In this section, you'll see the first of nineteen Bulletproof systems we've developed and shared with clients around the world. Each begins with a 'Trigger' – the event that brings the system or sub-system into play for a salesperson – and is followed by a 'Bulletproof Impact' – benefits the system brings to sales teams and in converting prospects to clients. Once we describe the impact of a system, we'll follow it with a 'Systemizing Success' section that walks sales leaders through creating that system for their own teams. While *Section I* addresses the systems we and our clients have found essential to drive sales meetings, *Section II* is a deep dive into what systems are possible to drive more impactful conversations with prospects, present more value than competitors, and close more deals.

In *Section III: Becoming Bulletproof*, we'll go over the powerful system used by the highest-performing teams in the world to ensure their systems remain dynamic, relevant, and keep up with the ever-changing environment salespeople operate in. This section will show salespeople how to incorporate what they learn in sales meetings – from prospect feedback and even information from other areas of the company – to ensure their systems remain Bulletproof. While any system can help a sales team be more successful at the time it's created, this section will ensure your sales systems remain up to date with your industry, prospect needs, and competitors. It will also give salespeople and sales leaders a way to ensure any new tactics or training they invest in is built into their existing systems, is consistently used, and actually yields a return.

Because Bulletproof selling is designed to improve the performance of both junior and veteran salespeople, leveraging the strengths each bring to the team, let's look at what actually comprises a sales system and understand why both our junior and veteran salespeople haven't systemized their sales.

SECTION I

*Systemizing
Sales*

CHAPTER 1

TRIMming Hope From Your Sales Strategy

WHILE MANY BOOKS have been written about sales tactics, processes, and strategies, few – if any – exist about how to turn those tools into *systems*. What made the people I studied around the world successful wasn't the fact that they'd been trained in the best processes. Many salespeople are provided with sales processes that are custom-made for their industry but are still not finding the success they're striving for.

The chief reason salespeople fall back on hope as their strategy isn't a lack of tools and processes, it's that they have no way to ensure those tools and processes are consistently used. Jeffrey Gittomer, a titan in the world of sales training, has often said, "Sales is a process." I don't disagree with him, but there's a difference between processes and systems. It's the latter that we'll be focusing on. So before we walk through how to systemize every aspect of your sales, from pipeline creation to prospecting to closing, we need to understand what a system is, and what it isn't.

Many sales leaders believe they have plenty of sales systems in place, and when results lag, they blame their salespeople for not using the systems they've provided. While complacent salespeople do exist, they don't tend to last long in the sales profession. When we interview salespeople, we find their systems aren't really systems. Instead, they're loosely defined processes that are occasionally used. It's no wonder so many sales leaders fall back on hope as their strategy.

To start, let's define what a sales system is, so as we work through the steps of standing up your own Bulletproof systems, you'll have an expert's insight into what makes a system different from a process, strategy, or tactic. Because we'll be 'trimming' hope from your sales strategy, it's only fitting that we use the acronym 'TRIM' to define a sales system.

T – Trigger

Every sales system must have a 'trigger' event, or some external event that brings the system into play. Whether it's researching a prospect, launching them into a sales campaign, prepping for a sales meeting, conducting a discovery session, or issuing a proposal, Bulletproof systems are linked to external events in a sales cycle. While a single system may serve multiple events, it's imperative that each system be tied to one or more trigger events so a salesperson knows to launch the system. This also ensures sales leaders can follow up with their salespeople to verify a particular system is being used with prospects.

For instance, if a system is created for debriefing sales meetings and 10 sales meetings are conducted in the course of a week, then 10 meeting debriefs should have been run as well.

Once a trigger event has occurred, the appropriate system is launched on a prospect's account so the salesperson can execute its steps. After sharing these insights with thousands of business leaders and salespeople, we've learned if a system does not have a trigger event associated with it, its likelihood of being used will be minimal.

As we explain the sales systems our clients have found most successful throughout this book, we'll also identify common trigger events that bring those sales systems into play.

R – Repeatable

A system that's not repeatable isn't a system, it's a fluke. As we work to identify the areas in your sales processes systems could benefit, we'll also need to ensure that the systems we create can be replicated across your prospects.

It does take time to create, stand up, and implement a sales system. Therefore, to ensure we get appropriate ROI (return on investment) from our systems, we must also ensure that we're standing up systems for the tasks our salespeople actually encounter in their sales cycles. The systems we walk through in this book cover the most common activities salespeople engage in, from prospecting to conducting sales meetings to generating referrals, but you'll also be encouraged to examine the other places in your business model that would benefit from creating systems.

One of the most critical and often overlooked parts of making a system repeatable is where it lives. A repeatable system is not dependent on a salesperson having to remember dozens of best practices. Rather, it can be called upon and used by any salesperson with access to it. This is why housing systems within the company CRM is a topic we'll cover throughout the book.

I – Improvable

One of the key differences between a Bulletproof sales system and a process is that most sales processes are static. Once they're created, salespeople are expected to use them until they're told to stop – and we've often found salespeople are rarely held accountable to use even the processes they're provided with. The systems we share in this book are based on systems used in the most dangerous and challenging places on earth: combat zones.

In those environments, static processes don't last long. The teams I studied regularly update their own systems so they could stay alive. The systems we'll be sharing throughout this book are all improvable and not meant to be written in stone. As economic changes, pandemics, or a new generation of salespeople and prospects enter the scene, systems that used to work often cause more harm for sales than good.

Throughout these pages, you will learn how to actively elicit feedback from your sales team and uncover gaps when they appear. There is also an entire chapter devoted to updating any sales systems that become out of date.

M – Measurable

Measuring systems applies in two areas: the efficacy of the system and how often its used.

First, sales leaders must be able to measure how many times any given system is being used. While this doesn't have to be actively tracked in the same way that deal conversion and time-to-close ratios are, it is important that sales leaders have the ability to monitor whether salespeople are using the systems they invested time in creating.

For instance, if a campaign is created for 'cold' prospects, sales leaders need to be able to measure how many prospects that campaign is used on. If salespeople didn't use the campaign system, we know we have a coaching problem. If the system was used on every new prospect entering our pipelines and we aren't happy with the results, we know we need to modify the campaign system.

Second, if a system does not produce measurable improvement in time saved, sales cycle shortened, or perhaps most importantly, sales made, then it's time to modify the system.

While systems are not new to the world of sales, there's a reason they're not as popular as they are in every other area of business. The top manufacturing companies on the planet couldn't live without their systems, and yet salespeople, for the most part, are unaware of the power systems can have in achieving their goals.

Let's take a look at why systems have taken so long to catch up to the world of sales, how sales teams are changing, and the reason systems are more important now than they've ever been.

CHAPTER 2

Why We Haven't Systemized Selling

IF YOU'RE A veteran of the sales industry, you're familiar with a curse that plagues the world of sales teams:

The *FNG*.

In family-friendly terms, that acronym stands for 'freaking new guy/gal,' and this type of salesperson is the bane of many sales managers' existence.

Regardless of the product or service being sold, sales success is largely dependent on getting in front of the right prospects at the right time. Each organization has a unique approach to doing this – in addition to the unique selling propositions of their products and services – and *all of it* has to be learned by new salespeople, who *hope* they'll remember it.

Perhaps without realizing it, *FNG*s understand the power of systems because they're built into every piece of technology this younger generation of salespeople grew up with. Unfortunately, because few sales organizations leverage systems, *FNG*s are largely unaware of the power systems can have in assisting with their sales goals.

There's another curse of the sales world: the *FOG*.

You might have guessed it – the *freaking old guy/gal*. Before I start getting hate mail accusing me of ageism, I'm not using 'old' to denote age. Instead, 'old' means 'stuck in an old way of doing things.'

This type of salesperson has acquired a lot of previous experience and innate sales processes across their careers, but rarely captures them and has even fewer ways to adapt them to changes that inevitably occur. Like the *FNG*, hope plays a major role in the *FOG's* sales strategy as well.

Veteran salespeople may have decades of experience responding to objections, as well as overcoming the challenges of finding prospects, qualifying them, getting appointments, and driving buying decisions. They hope they can repeat their success on their next sales call. That equals *hundreds*, if not *thousands*, of hard-earned lessons they and their sales managers hope they don't have to relearn with the next prospect.

If you're wondering if there are *FOGs* amongst your salespeople, ask them to show you their pipeline in the CRM your company uses. If you don't *have* a CRM and you're in charge of managing salespeople, *you* might be the *FOG*. Don't worry, it's not a terminal diagnosis. If a senior salesperson doesn't have a pipeline or don't/won't/can't use their CRMs, you have at least one *FOG* on your hands.

Unfortunately, every industry on the planet is changing, which means the way we sell must be updated at least as fast as our industries change. In fact, if we want more market share as those changes occur, we must adapt *faster* than the rate of change.

There is a way to solve both of these problems simultaneously – getting *FNGs* the lessons they'll need faster than they could through their own experience and getting *FOGs* engaged in leveraging technology to apply the lessons they've learned from a lifetime of selling – all while replacing hope with certainty.

The solution to bringing your *FOGs* up to speed and getting your *FNGs* producing? Systems.

Standing up sales systems, whether you're a team of one or 1,000, comes from a desire to not only help our sales today but to ensure we're preparing ourselves – and our companies – for sales success in the future. That comes from a culture of fanatically implementing best practices and asking, "What about the next team in?"

What About the Next Team In?

After clearing a city block of houses, returning from a foot patrol, or escorting a high-level official through dangerous territory, Marines would always take the time to thoroughly examine what went well on their missions and what didn't.

For Marines clearing houses, this meant a report on every risk they encountered: dangerous entrances, blind corners, and even suspicious-looking debris on the ground. I asked one of them once, "Why do you take the time to capture all that when you've just been ordered into another section of the city and probably won't come back to that house again?"

It was answered with such gravity I never had to ask the question more than once. The battle-hardened warrior turned to me and asked, "What about the next team in?"

Because of the dangerous nature of their work, these men and women needed every advantage to improve their chances of survival. That meant not only ensuring *they* performed well, but also included setting the teams that came behind them up for success. Unfortunately, sharing best practices happens far too little in most sales teams.

An effect of nurturing this 'What About the Next Team In?' sales culture is that team members go out looking for information to share with the 'next team in.' That may look like recording information on the prospect they're pursuing in their CRM, or it might look like capturing what to do or what to avoid in future sales conversations based on what they learned.

A salesperson with a 'next team in' mentality moves from being reactive, responding to whatever is happening during a sales call, to proactive, looking for ways to adapt and innovate to increase sales, prepare future team members for success, and better serve their clients.

Many salespeople reading this will no doubt be cocking an eyebrow, ready to tell me in vehement emails and spammy LinkedIn messages how *they* are successful without needing systems. Whether you're a salesperson, entrepreneur, or sales manager, let's look at the difference between a Bulletproof salesperson and one relying on hope. See which category, based on the below criteria, you or your team fits in across the stages of your sales cycle:

Bulletproof Salespeople	Salespeople Living on Hope
Finding Prospects: Continually refine lead qualification to expand their pipeline and reach new markets	**Finding Prospects:** Take leads as they come, hoping enough inbound referrals and inquiries appear
Schedule time each day or week for adding new prospects into outreach	Hope there is time to reach out to prospects when everything else is done
Research *every* prospect before outreach, learning about their business or industry to customize offering	Hopes they'll remember similar prospects' challenges when making first contact
Outreach: Use a script refined each week to drive meetings, overcome objections, and discover information needed to move a deal further through the pipeline	**Outreach:** Script? Might have one of those somewhere. Hasn't been updated in a while and few people use it. Hope prospects give them enough information to move deals forward
Sales Conversation: Brief beforehand with a supervisor, follow a structured format with	**Sales Conversation:** Happen when they happen, but account history rarely reviewed. Hope salespeople

options, customizations, and pricing prepped beforehand	know what they're doing when selling
Negotiations: Enters sales conversations knowing their prospect's likely budget range and have a list of options prepped for discussion at various price points	**Negotiations:** Hope prospect has budget and that if they negotiate, hope they don't leave too much on the table
Learning from Sales Meetings: Debrief sales meetings to ensure all points were covered and capture anything learned that could improve sales in the future	**Learning from Sales Meetings:** Why would salespeople share anything? Hope salespeople learn from mistakes and repeat successes
Product or service Delivery: Remain an active participant in the client's adoption of the product or service, learning from them what could be done better with selling *and* product or service delivery to provide for an improved client experience and increased sales in the future	**Product or service Delivery:** Uninvolved after the sale, client handed off to an account manager. Hope their company serves the client well
Referral Generation: Actively solicit referrals from customers in a structured way, leveraging organic and online networks to facilitate introductions	**Referral Generation:** If a client is happy, isn't it up to them to refer others? Hope referrals happen

As you can see, there is a *massive* difference from the way a Bulletproof salesperson goes about their sales activities and the way someone relying on hope operates. If you're a salesperson and wonder how all the things in the column on the left *happen consistently*, this book is your guide.

Whether you're part of an established sales team or standing one up from scratch, we'll need to find a place for your processes to live before we begin to convert them into Bulletproof systems.

CHAPTER 3

One System To Rule Them All

You do not rise to the level of your goals. You fall to the level of your systems. -James Clear, in his book Atomic Habits

BUT WAIT, MANY salespeople and sales managers will say, what we're doing is generating revenue, so it must work!

If money is coming in, why is it critical we still take the time to systemize our sales? Systems allow us to turn a pattern into a repeatable event. Here's how we know if you're leveraging systems or whether your current sales are simply the result of a pattern:

If you were called out of action today, could another salesperson pick up **all** of your accounts and continue right along with those prospects' sales cycles, knowing what the next point of scheduled outreach was, when it should occur, by what communication channel, and what that next message should communicate?

Do the strategies you use to overcome objections live somewhere that your team can review and learn from?

Have you captured the reason for every lost sale and have a written plan to prevent sales being lost for those reasons again?

In all the time you've been selling, how often do you review your sales systems, ensuring they're keeping up with technology and changes in your industry? Have you ever?

Bulletproof teams, whether clearing a house or selling a product or service, do. all of the above things on a regular basis. That's what defines something as a Bulletproof sales system: It lives outside the heads of salespeople and is simple enough for someone else to execute with proper training.

Even sales teams with processes may unknowingly be basing them on hope because few processes are regularly re-examined. Adaptable systems, by definition, can't be static. What keeps sales systems dynamic and up to date with market changes is the fact that they are continually examined, refined, and improved. We'll go over exactly how to do that in this book, but there's an old management adage worth revisiting before we convert any processes you have into Bulletproof systems:

Making a broken system more efficient produces more broken results.

Making a subpar sales process faster and more efficient may produce more sales in the short-term, but it will inevitably crash and burn when the next market shift or pandemic occurs. If we're building a system that can both produce sales and withstand changing markets and industry shifts, we need to take a closer look at the overarching system that allows us to build triggers so we, and our salespeople, will know which systems to bring into effect on prospects at specific times.

Until recently, there hasn't been a way for salespeople to create systems that lived outside their heads. It's why hope became the strategy for even well-trained sales teams. Fortunately, there's a platform that is tailor-made for capturing and refining sales systems. For the *Lord of the Rings* fans out there, this is the 'one system to rule them all.' Conveniently, it's an inexpensive software platform that goes by a simple three-letter acronym.

The brevity of these three letters can't possibly communicate the value this platform can have to your own sales team in becoming Bulletproof:

CRM. Customer Relationship Management.

If the combat teams I was with had something akin to a CRM tool, it would look like a searchable database of every house in a neighborhood, along with maps of the roads, addresses of houses scheduled for clearing, timetables for clearing them, blueprints of those house's layouts, and a profile of everyone in every house they were likely to encounter – all available in an app on the teams' iPhones. To say such a resource would have saved lives and made these high-performing teams even *more* effective is an understatement. And yet, every salesperson on the planet can have such a resource at their fingertips – often provided and paid for by the company they're selling for.

When I began my own journey in sales, I did what most entrepreneurs do and bootstrapped everything, including my bootstraps. To manage a growing list of prospects, I used a mix of Google contacts, an Excel spreadsheet, and a Gmail account. That worked when I was tracking a dozen prospects, but quickly become unwieldy. And that was just for basic communication, not running dynamic selling systems!

There came a point when I had to invest in a platform that was designed to help me facilitate what I was trying to accomplish: managing customer relationships.

Once I had a CRM and spent a few hours setting it up, loading contacts, and tagging them, I had all my prospects in a database that was outside of my head. I could now schedule outreach to prospects via email, phone, LinkedIn, and direct mail. But then questions arose that most salespeople face in establishing outreach:

How often should I reach out? By what methods?

Should I contact some groups of prospects more than others?

Is there a better time of year for me to be in contact with some prospects?

Larger questions also appeared, questions that few business owners or salespeople know to ask to better leverage their CRMs:

How can I use the information in this CRM to make better business decisions?

Is there a way to predict revenue month-by-month from the data in here?

Can I use my account notes to design better products, services, and improve the way I sell, as well as expanding who I sell to?

Of course, the data in a CRM can answer all those questions and many more. By using a database that is shared *across* an organization whether you're a sales team of one or 1,000, you have the ability to learn from one another, prevent lost sales in the future, and increase revenue with future deals.

In today's business landscape, if we don't learn from each other and work together to improve the value we provide to clients, there's a plethora of younger, more nimble competitors who are happy to serve our customers in the ways they need help *today*. For those of us running our own businesses, if we don't both learn from our own sales mistakes and have the ability to reference those lessons in the future, we're bound to repeat some or all of them.

As I began to grow in my own capabilities with my CRM and worked with companies to grow theirs, I realized that even basic CRMs can be used as day-by-day barometers of business health. Sales leaders can create campaign or template changes that scale across all their salespeople's CRMs that affect long-term results in prospect response and therefore, revenue.

Why do I place so much emphasis on what is, in effect, a database?

The Power of Information

I don't want to give the impression that elite military teams don't have sophisticated technology – some travel with millions of dollars' worth of training in their heads and equipment on their backs – but they also have access to databases that save lives. These databases are not advanced and artificial intelligence-based, at least as of this writing. Instead, they're much more basic and perhaps infinitely more valuable because of it.

Think back across your own history in sales to *every sale that wasn't made*. If you've been selling longer than a week, you likely have more of these than you care to remember: every phone call that went nowhere, every in-person visit that didn't close, every proposal that was modified or rejected by a prospect, every instance where financing fell through, and every time a client didn't give you solid testimonials and referrals to pursue.

There may be hundreds of individual instances, if not thousands, for every salesperson in your organization.

Imagine if you had a database with a running count of every lost deal in your company, why it was lost, what the salesperson learned from it, and what should be done differently in the future with similar prospects. Not just that, but this database also had records of every won deal, why it was won, and what the salesperson learned from the situation that other salespeople could repeat in the future.

Would you close more deals? Would you generate more revenue for yourself and your company with access to that information?

As a sales manager, do you think your sales team would perform better if *everyone* had access to that information from past won and lost deals, from data updated every week?

It would be a gamechanger for any sales team – and for the first time, this book makes that system available to the world of sales.

Bulletproof selling systems run the gamut of our prospect's buying stages and sales cycle. Buying stages often define a system's 'trigger' and denote which Bulletproof systems should be applied at what time.

The verticals that live within your CRM are commonly referred to as a *pipeline*, and building a pipeline is where we'll start in making your sales Bulletproof.

CHAPTER 4

Pipelines Aren't Just For Plumbers

The pipe is life. – Jeb Blount

THE PERFORMANCE OF a great team – whether on the battlefield or in athletics – often seems choreographed. It seems as if everyone knew where each of their teammates and opponents was, where they were going to be, accounted for it, and were able to adjust accordingly.

Ask these teams if they actually *had* choreographed their movements and you'll get a confusing answer:

Yes *and* No.

Yes, they spent hours, or years, practicing for that type of scenario, that type of situation in that type of environment.

And no, they hadn't choreographed those movements because they'd never been in that *exact* place, on that field or in that building, with the exact team members or the exact competitors moving in the same way.

Yet we all marvel at a team moving together as a cohesive unit. How does it happen? How do Bulletproof teams communicate in a way that allows them to operate together seamlessly and still innovate solutions that look like they'd been practiced forever?

The Bulletproof teams I was fortunate enough to study in person weren't comprised exclusively of Mensa-level geniuses, but they didn't have to be. They were trained in systems honed over decades to ensure they were as effective as they could be for the type of environment and situation their users would be stepping into.

Many of us in sales have shared a marketing or sales tactic with a peer and wondered why it didn't stick. Or perhaps we learned a great outreach idea from a book or sales training program and hoped we would remember it when reaching out to our next prospect, but found it was quickly forgotten.

The solution is something most entrepreneurs are unaware of and most businesses ignore when planning prospect outreach:

Campaign Systems.

All campaign systems, even the ones we'll share in this book, can be housed, maintained, and quickly updated with a CRM. If a CRM can house all of our campaign (outreach) systems, how do we know how to set triggers to bring certain campaigns into play at specific times?

This is where a pipeline comes in. Pipelines are called that because they track the flow of a prospect through the course of their sales cycle. While many salespeople are familiar with the model of a sales funnel that filters prospects from a wide point at the top to the narrow point at the bottom where some convert into customers, the differences between a funnel and a pipeline are critical for a Bulletproof salesperson to understand.

Funnels are designed for putting a large group of potential prospects into, with only a few becoming customers. That works well if you're not sure if the folks you're pursuing are qualified buyers. For those salespeople spending time qualifying prospects, funnels are an invitation for prospect attrition, wasted time, and missed sales goals. It's not entirely the fault of the funnel, however. Sales funnels are built on the premise of hoping enough prospects convert into clients. This comes from the mistaken belief that we only need one funnel, or series of outreach steps, for all prospects, regardless of what we know about the prospect or where that prospect is in their sales cycle. In other words, using a single funnel to jam all our leads into is just yet another way of relying on hope as a sales strategy.

Why?

Most funnels leak more prospects than they convert, an unfortunate flaw of a funnel's design. If a company could convert every prospect that simply interacted with their brand, it wouldn't require a sales force and *should* be an e-commerce company.

Where a pipeline differentiates itself from a sales funnel is that pipeline stages can be constructed to handle prospects in dozens of scenarios, each specially built to convert a prospect in that stage of the buying cycle into a customer. And it can all be constructed within your CRM.

Many *FOG*s will justify their hatred of CRMs and all predefined outreach cadences by declaring that each deal must be handled uniquely because each customer is unique, and that logic is valid. However, I have yet to encounter an industry where prospects didn't fit into basic categories as they advanced from 'never having heard about the product or service' to 'being interested' to 'in active sales conversations' to 'client.' Because of this, it is possible to construct deal stages within a pipeline that are unique to your customers, industry, and product or service. Instead of forcing salespeople to shoehorn leads into a single outreach funnel, using a pipeline turns sales systems from a one-dimensional process (a funnel) into a three-dimensional system (a pipeline). Each deal stage of a pipeline contains an outreach campaign that, in turn, defines specific outreach steps to conduct with each prospect in that stage of their buying cycle.

Leveraging a pipeline with campaign systems is the *opposite* of using hope as a sales strategy.

Many of our clients, once they learn the value a pipeline has for a sales team, choose to construct pipelines for each area of their business' operations – marketing, production, distribution, customer service, etc. While we won't focus on replicating sales pipelines into non-sales functions in this book, know that having an at-a-glance map of the flow of customers through touchpoints in a company's processes can do wonders for the sanity of any sales manager or CEO.

Map Your Pipeline by Defining Your Prospect's Journey

Harvey Mackay, another sales trainer who's been sharing tactics and processes with generations of salespeople, has a story he likes to share about asking an old, grizzled sales veteran when it was OK to quit reaching out to an unresponsive prospect. The grizzled veteran replied, "When they die, or you die."

At first glance, that story simply encourages salespeople to be persistent. But persistence is not enough in today's world. Calling a prospect every week for years may not yield a sale – but might generate a restraining order. Additionally, that type of fanatical follow-up may be possible with a few prospects but quickly becomes unwieldy when scaled across dozens or hundreds of prospects. The question is, how do we *systemize* persistence over a period of time? And how do we scale that across hundreds or thousands of prospects?

Although physicists and plumbers will balk at the analogy I'm about to share, bear with me for a few minutes as it reveals the power a pipeline can have in systemizing the level of persistence Harvey recommends.

Imagine you're visiting the construction site of a new house and you have a clear view of the plumbing pipes as they're being installed. You'll notice at least one inlet into the plumbing – the water source, either from a nearby well or the local utility. Now imagine there are no outlets in this house's plumbing system. No drains, toilets, sinks, or any way for the water to leave once it enters. In this imaginary house, pipes are built with a futuristic material that can hold an unlimited amount of water and prevent backflow into the inlet, no matter how much water is allowed in.

When the inlet valve is opened, water rushes into the pipes and begins to circulate. Because there's no outlet and the water can't leave, it continues to circulate. And keeps circulating.

Here's how that would look:

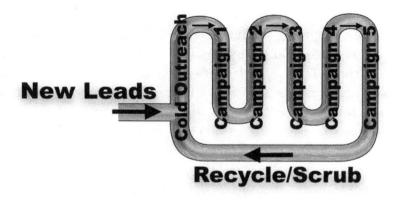

When you put prospects into a pipeline like the one shown here, you've created a closed-circuit system where prospects will be kept 'circulating' until date-specific reminders trigger prospects to come back in front of you and your salespeople for action.

This solves the problem many salespeople face with attrition of qualified prospects in their pipelines. With a closed pipeline in place that has set dates to bring every qualified account back into play, we don't have to hope we remember to contact prospects.

To begin mapping your pipeline, first ask: What are the 'buckets' a prospect *and/or* client could be in at each stage of their buying cycle? I include clients in this model because predictable referral generation *should* be part of systemized sales campaigns. Referrals can come from prospects, but most organizations' own clients are an overlooked source of continuous referrals.

For our clients, we recommend these as a basic outline for pipeline verticals or deal stages:

Not A Fit Right Now	Could Not Reach	Cold Out-reach	Decision Maker Identified	Pre-select	Active Oppor-tunity	Won Deal	Lost Deal

Below is a brief explanation of what each of those verticals represent, as well as the next step in each if a vertical's campaign fails to convert a prospect into a customer:

Not a Fit Right Now: This vertical is for prospects or former clients who have told us they're not doing business for a set period of time. This could be indicated by a lack of response to outreach attempts or due to contractual obligations, preferred vendor relationships, lack of minimum budget, or a slew of other issues. Prospects flow here from either the Could Not Reach campaign or when we hear 'no' or 'not now' in a buyer conversation that can't be overcome. This vertical is one of the two 'holding tanks' in the pipeline, meaning that an account could potentially sit here with only passive outreach attempts (monthly newsletters, etc.) until they are ready to enter an active outreach campaign system again.

Next Step for Prospects from This Vertical: At a predetermined date in the future, re-qualify prospects in this stage and get them into the Cold Outreach campaign system or Decision Maker Identified campaign system.

Could Not Reach: This vertical is for prospects who haven't responded to outreach attempts but are worth additional pursuit before removing them from our pipelines or putting them into a holding tank for a few months before restarting outreach. Like all outreach campaign systems, it is designed to get the prospect into active communication and drive a sales conversation. Prospects flow here from the Cold Outreach or Decision Maker Identified verticals.

Next Step for Prospects from This Vertical: If this campaign fails to generate a conversation with a decision maker and move the account into one of the more 'valuable' campaign systems, move the account to the Not A Fit Right Now vertical with a firm follow-up date to get it back into play.

Cold Outreach: This is the campaign we use when a prospect has never heard of us or we've been out of contact long enough that they likely don't remember us. Prospects enter this campaign from warm referrals (where we don't have direct contact to a confirmed decision maker), cold leads, or from the Not A Fit Right Now holding tank.

Next Step for Prospects from This Vertical: If this campaign system doesn't get us the information we need to move the sale forward or at least identify the decision maker, the prospect's account flows to the Could Not Reach campaign system.

Decision Maker Identified: This is the campaign we use when we have confirmed a decision maker (someone with fiduciary authority to make a decision about the product or service we sell). It is also designed to drive a sales conversation or get the account into Preselect if a buying decision cannot be made at that time due to budgets, purchase periods, etc.

Next Step for Prospects from This Vertical: If this campaign fails to generate a conversation with a decision maker or fails to yield us the information we need to get the account into Preselect, it flows to the Could Not Reach campaign. It bypasses the Cold Outreach campaign because the purpose of that initial campaign has already been achieved: we know who the decision maker is.

Preselect: The most valuable campaign; this is where qualified accounts who could not make a buying decision for a variety of reasons are held until they enter their buying window. This is the other 'holding tank' in the pipeline because significant time may pass between a conversation with a prospect and when their buying window occurs/their Preselect campaign becomes active. Because we can set dates for future tasks within a CRM, each of the accounts within this vertical can be programmed to come back in front of the salesperson managing the account when the prospect is in their buying window. Due to the qualified budget of these accounts and known decision makers, its campaign system often justifies more expensive outreach efforts.

Next Step for Prospects from This Vertical: If our outreach attempts are ignored in Preselect, the account flows to the Decision Maker Identified vertical for another attempt at the sales conversation or discovering the next buying window, which would then put it back into the holding tank of Preselect with a future date for outreach.

Active Opportunity: This vertical isn't a campaign as much as it is a series of tasks to complete when engaged in active sales conversations or when waiting for proposals to be executed: sales meeting briefs, sales conversations, and post-meeting debriefs, all systems we'll explore later. This vertical allows us, at a glance, to see not only what accounts are closest to becoming customers but also potential deal values that we can use in predicting future sales once we know our conversion ratios.

Next Step for Prospects from This Vertical: If the account converts to a sale, it is placed in the Won Deal vertical for service delivery and referral generation. If the opportunity is lost, it is placed in the Lost Deal campaign.

Won Deal: This is where active clients in our pipeline live, so the salesperson who closed the deal can keep them top of mind throughout the year. Remember: the best referrals are from satisfied customers.

Next Step for Prospects from This Vertical: If an account stops being a customer or cycles out after service delivery, this account would then flow to Decision Maker Identified for requalification into a sales conversation for additional services or into Preselect for purchasing our product or service in the future.

Lost Deal: This campaign is where Active Opportunities end up when a deal is lost to a competitor or no purchase decision is made. This is perhaps one of the most valuable stages in the pipeline for a Bulletproof salesperson. We advise salespeople with prospects in this vertical to discover why the deal was lost and build that feedback into Lessons Learned, a topic we've devoted a whole chapter to.

Next Step for Prospects from This Vertical: From this vertical, a prospect ideally moves into Preselect as we discover what could have been done differently to win the sale next time and determine the next buying timeframe.

If CRMs and pipelines are new to you, don't concern yourself too much with the technical aspects of pipeline verticals and CRM setup. The *how* of their setup is something every CRM technical support team can walk you through once you're a customer of their platform. The most important thing to take away from the concept of pipeline verticals is that unless we can see where our prospects are across buying stages, it's impossible to know whether we have forward or backward movement in our pipeline or whether our campaigns systems are successfully moving prospects towards becoming customers.

The most valuable attribute of defining buying stages and assigning a multi-step campaign system to each of those verticals is we don't have to think about what happens next with any prospect, regardless of where they are in their buying journey; the system handles the trigger for the next type of outreach on the cadence we define ahead of time.

Why is engineering a prospect's sales journey this valuable – *and this necessary* – to create a Bulletproof selling system?

Your sales calls won't result in an exchange of gunfire, but your sales situations will still be stressful, challenging, and can blow up before they even begin. It makes sense to free you and your sales team up from trying to manage next steps across hundreds or thousands of prospects so they can focus on what counts: being present with the next prospect they reach out to.

As you brainstorm what your pipeline and its verticals might look like in your industry, ask yourself these questions:

1. *What are the 'stages' my prospects could be in on their way to becoming a customer?*
2. *For each stage, what do I need to know about or from the prospect at that point in the sales cycle to move the account forward in the future if they can't buy today?*
3. *If the campaign system doesn't work or the prospect is unresponsive, what stage of the pipeline would be the next logical fit for the prospect?*

Before we begin systemizing our prospecting by constructing campaign systems for each deal stage of our pipelines, we'll need to understand *what* we'll be communicating to our prospects to drive meetings and buying decisions. That begins with systemizing our messaging, its mediums, and its cadence to ensure our salespeople are using best practices in prospecting and communicating the value of your product or service within each of your campaign systems.

SECTION II

Sales
Systems

CHAPTER 5

Systemizing Value

A MAJOR PART of the Marines' jobs in Iraq was to patrol local neighborhoods and keep them secure. Our opponents quickly realized they could do more damage to our personnel by avoiding direct engagements and simply planting explosive devices on the side of the roads we traveled on. Less risk to them, more risk to us.

Because a 40-millimeter mortar round with a bunch of colorful wires laying on the side of the road is a clear indication of danger, these improvised explosive devices would often be camouflaged. This made them hard to spot and led to a lot of false-positive identifications. If something looked like a disguised bomb, we'd halt an entire convoy to investigate. A patrol could be held up for hours because the lead driver spotted something that *could* be a problem.

What happened next in these situations was no less impressive than watching a team of snipers clear a building – troops would unload from their vehicles and take up defensive positions on either side of the road, run to the tops of nearby buildings, and do everything they could to proactively meet a potential ambush.

And then we'd wait. For what? For the Explosive Ordnance Disposal (EOD) team to arrive. These men and women had the especially dangerous job of getting close enough to confirm whether what we spotted was indeed a bomb. If so, their job was disarming it or blowing it in place. They were masters of communicating and leveraging their value – something that many salespeople have replaced with product specs and pricing sheets as their primary sales tools.

Thinking back, watching these EOD teams work was the first time I saw how a salesperson could assess the situation, recommend value-added solutions, and get to work delivering them in a systemized way.

If these EOD technicians had been like most salespeople, they would chat all of us up upon arrival until they discovered who had the most rank, and then negotiations would begin, whereupon we'd all be regaled with the history of bomb disposal. Then the EOD team would open up their bag of goodies and display all the ways they could disarm a bomb or destroy it. At that point, they'd select their tools and get to work. Once done, they'd offer the bomb as a souvenir to the decision maker so they'd have a memento of the great work the bomb disposal team had done. And of course, before departing, they'd be sure to ask if the convoy commander knew of any other units in the area that might be encountering bombs so the EOD team could … you know … get referrals.

That would turn what should be a half-hour mission into a multi-day affair. The EOD teams figured out something vitally important salespeople should remember when communicating with prospects – no one cares about *how* something solves a major problem. What folks care about is how *fast and effectively* the problem can be solved. Unless speed and effectiveness are impacted, it does not make sense to talk about upgrades, upsells, or which colors something comes in.

What *actually* happened when the bomb disposal team arrived to one of our halted patrols? And what can our salespeople do to model the way they communicated value?

First, the EOD team would immediately locate and speak with the ranking officer, ensure troops were pushed out to a safe distance in case of an intended or unintended detonation, and confirm that civilians were cordoned off from the potential

41

blast area. Then, the team would get to work providing the benefit they existed to provide: allow the mission, in this case the patrol, to be accomplished as quickly and safely as possible.

The EOD teams were Bulletproof salespeople, even though they'd rightly claim to be experts at simply blowing stuff up.

If that example doesn't get you thinking about how to connect your salespeople with the value your company exists to provide, here's another:

Linda is a solopreneur and running a nutritional consultancy, a fancy way of saying she teaches people what to eat and drink in order to perform better. One of her prospects was the local police department, but she was having trouble convincing their police chief to let her present to his officers. The police officers were busy, worked in a stressful job, and were infinitely more concerned with staying on the right side of the law than they were with what they ate in their patrol vehicles, donut jokes aside.

When I asked Linda what the benefit of her talk was, she began telling me about how eating refined sugar led to early onset diabetes, poor energy levels, etc. I encouraged her to think of this from the perspective of her decision maker – the person with the ability to cut a check for nutritional advice.

I asked, "What is top of mind for a police chief, the things they think about and are most concerned with?"

Some answers she came up with:

Following policies and procedures during traffic stops

Maintain proficiency with weapons and arrest techniques

Abiding by HR policies

"Those are good," I told Linda, "but let's go deeper. What's the one thing that could happen in the course of a given day that would ruin a police chief's mood even if everything else went right?"

She decided that obviously, it would be if one or more of their officers didn't make it home.

"Right!" I said. "And can you link nutrition to better decision-making, enhanced focus, response time, and better memory?"

"Yes!" she replied.

"Great, then *that's* the value you're talking about the next time you speak to the police chief – increasing the chances all their officers survive their next shift."

No surprise, she got the gig.

What happened was not magic; it was simply examining the benefits of the service she offered, not from *her* perspective but from the perspective of her *prospect*. She needed to identify the biggest need of her prospect and build a bridge from her expertise, product, or service to that goal.

Systemizing Value

Trigger: Standing up a Bulletproof campaign system.

Bulletproof Impact of This System: Understanding how your product or service creates change in your clients' lives and businesses. Allows your salespeople to expand their potential customer profile across industries, identify the most pressing need in their prospect's lives, and position your product or service as a solution. Overcomes the 'show up and throw up' method of selling and positions salespeople for strategically oriented, solutions-based sales.

This is an exercise that is *essential* for entrepreneurs and those providing intangible services, but it's also valuable for product-based sales teams to examine the actual value provided by what they sell. It's these value statements that will form the bulk of sales scripts, generate discovery questions, and improve the closing ratio of proposals (all systems we'll reveal in coming chapters).

It's an old adage that people don't buy features – they buy benefits. Yet few sales teams, and even fewer solopreneurs, take the time to define the value their product or service provides, and even fewer prioritize communicating that value in their sales conversations. Because we're preparing salespeople for the most challenging environments they might encounter, it's not enough to just train them on remembering product specs. They need to be versed on the solutions their products or services provide and be able to communicate them to busy, distracted decisions makers. Instead of assuming prospects want to know all the *features* of a product or service, Bulletproof salespeople take the time to learn about their prospects' needs first. Only when a clear match between prospects' goals and a way their product or service can deliver the solution is identified should salespeople attempt to sell.

Let's examine how to do that for what you're selling so we can get to the heart of the value your company's products or services provide. That value will be woven into all of the sales conversations, outreach systems, templates, and marketing material that we'll walk you through creating in upcoming chapters.

Start by mapping out the below columns and their titles on the top of a sheet of paper. Set aside an entire sheet as you'll need the space:

Features	Specifications	Benefits

In the 'features' column, write down everything you or your salespeople would normally say if someone requested, "Tell me about yourself and what you sell." This includes the life story of the salesperson, your company's founder, the history of the product or service, the way it was smuggled across a battlefield to keep it from falling into enemy hands in the big war, etc. This is the column salespeople tend to spend the most time in when speaking with prospects, and it's not an effective way to capture attention or move a sale forward. Prospects sometimes will buy something just so the salesperson will *stop talking about features*. Most, however, will say, "Leave me your information and we'll get back to you."

In the second column, write the specifications of your product or service – just the facts. Salespeople often spend time memorizing dozens of these on the off chance someone will want to know how many cubic feet of floor space their widget takes up. While specs are valuable, they're nothing that can't be kept on a reference sheet. For service providers, this column would contain all the *ways* they provide their services or communicate their expertise for their clients: consulting, speeches, coaching, counseling, training, advising, etc.

It's the third column where Bulletproof salespeople live. To fill in this column for the product or service(s) you sell, ask yourself and your team, "How are our clients better off as the result of column one or column two?"

Top-line responses to this question usually include answers like more money or less problems for our clients, but it's essential to dive deeper. Follow up with any initial responses by asking, "And how does *that* look in the lives and businesses of the people we sell to?"

That second layer of responses will uncover how what you sell benefits your client's particular businesses and lives. But the benefits don't stop there. The third and final layer of this line of questioning for items in the third column is asking, "And what does *that* allow them to do that they wouldn't be able to do otherwise?"

Here's an example of this system's flow:

Question 1: "How are our clients better off with our widget?"

Answer 1: "It saves them money and allows them to produce more gadgets at a faster rate."

Question 2: "How does that look in the lives and businesses of the people we deliver widgets to?"

Answer 2: "They usually increase production 20%, making them more money. They get fewer defects which saves them a few hundred grand a year in return costs as well."

Question 3: "And what has that allowed them to do that they wouldn't be able to do otherwise?"

Answer 3: "Well, one of our clients was able to sell their business because of an increased valuation. Another was able to hire enough people to establish a third shift and created more jobs in their community. Someone else won an industry award and was featured in their association's magazine because they out-produced everyone else."

'Producing more widgets' is a commodity that is available through multiple channels, whatever the industry. 'Increasing company valuation while hiring more employees and being recognized as best-of-class in the industry' is something not everyone can provide – and something folks will pay a premium for, especially if they've expressed an interest in those outcomes!

As we'll share throughout this book, Bulletproof salespeople become Bulletproof because they don't position their product or service as a commodity, but rather as something that solves critical issues their prospects and clients face. For that reason, once we identify that we are speaking with a decision maker, we encourage salespeople to be familiar with how what they sell solves strategic problems.

Systemizing Success with Systemized Value

The messaging that your team will be building throughout their Bulletproof campaign systems and call scripts comes from that third line of questioning, which is why we're addressing the value of your product or service before we get into building campaign systems within your pipeline. For now, capture the ways your clients' businesses and lives are better with your product or service from your own experience or by surveying your sales and customer support teams.

Before we begin communicating our value to prospects within campaign systems, outreach scripts, or messaging templates, it's important to know that not all communication is created equally or has equal impact. Devoting too much time communicating value via email will not yield us the same result as dedicating time to making calls or through in-person appointments.

It's often said that nothing happens in business until something is sold. I'll add to that – nothing is sold until something is communicated. That makes communication the chief role of any salesperson, regardless of their product, service, prospect, or deal size.

An outreach system that converts meetings and sales relies on effective *communication,* because without it, sales don't happen. To make selling systems predictable, scalable, and continuously improving – or Bulletproof – we need to understand the types of communication available and the power they each have. Only then can we effectively leverage each type of communication as we build or revamp our pipelines and their outreach campaigns.

The 3 Levels of Bulletproof Communication

Have you ever met someone who tried to sell you something you wanted – and could afford – but you just couldn't convince yourself to pull the trigger on the item or service?

It's happened to all of us, and while many of us can't explain why we didn't make the purchase when need and budget were aligned, we can find a common denominator in every instance: the salesperson.

While many folks are excellent at memorizing product specs or managing huge professional networks, neither of those closes sales. On the other hand, we can all remember instances when we weren't aware of the need for a product or service and didn't have the budget, but still purchased something anyway. Again, the salesperson is often the common denominator.

The salespeople that communicate well will always be able to establish rapport faster and more effectively than those who stumble through their pitch, appear unsure of what they're saying, or give off untrustworthy signals. It's salespeople who present well in person that are in highest demand across industries, and for good reason. They've mastered the first and most valuable level of communication that forms the bulk of Bulletproof selling's outreach:

Person-To-Person Communication

It's this level of communication that involves the most subtleties: eye contact, body language, vocal tone, mirroring, and all the intricacies of human communication, even when meeting via video. The reason it's vital to know or be reminded of the value of person-to-person communication is that so many organizations build their outreach systems without making their most powerful form of communication primary.

While it may not be possible to visit each prospect, or even conduct sales negotiations in person, the efficacy of person-to-person communication should always play heavily in campaign systems. If you're lucky enough to be in an industry where your prospects and customers are geographically close, this means injecting as many person-to-person visits or virtual sessions as possible in your outreach steps. Online meeting platforms can substitute as a solution for geographical separation with prospects, but until holograms become affordable, face-to-face meetings – whether through visits or through video – will reign supreme in sales.

The second, and next most-valuable, level of communication is where most successful salespeople have learned to play:

Verbal Communication

Whether through inside sales or a combination of in-person visits and phone calls, a salesperson's voice is one of their most valuable sales assets. While phone-driven 'cold calls' are becoming rarer as the ability to research prospects increases, voice should still play an important role in any salesperson's outreach.

For those of us in industries that don't require hopping in vehicles or on airplanes to visit prospects, phone calls are how we develop relationships, field discovery questions, and close deals. Regardless of your industry, do not neglect voice as a powerful sales asset, and ensure vocal communication through phone calls weighs more heavily than email or written communication throughout all your campaign systems.

Finally, the third and least-valuable method of communication for a Bulletproof salesperson is:

Written Communication

While many salespeople consider themselves adept at writing sales copy, most elements of communication can't be expressed in even the best-written email or website page. While many people across industries are moving to email-only sales campaigns and hoping for a thin slice of a conversion percentage for future customers, they're doing themselves and their clients a disservice by relying on only one form of communication given it's the one least likely to generate relationships.

I'm not advocating avoiding email – we devote an entire section of this book to building systems for email communication and how to systemize email templates, but written communication shouldn't outweigh the more powerful types of outreach available: person-to-person and verbal.

Most *FOG*s are generating sales conversations not because they're that dang good; it's because they've established enough rapport with accounts that they are comfortable relying on verbal communication. What gets them that level of comfort in developing those relationships?

They're unconsciously using a series of outreach processes they've learned throughout their careers. Unfortunately, those are processes *FOG*s picked up by getting it wrong at *least* once with a past prospect. The next chapter will show us how to build powerful campaign systems that will ensure our *FOG*s don't have to hope they remember everything they've learned when prospecting and our *FNG*s don't have to learn every outreach lesson the hard way.

CHAPTER 6

Campaign Systems

Prospecting is a campaign, not an event - Anthony Iannarino

ANTHONY'S QUOTE IS worth diving into before we explore the mechanics of creating campaign systems. Too many salespeople will receive or research a lead, reach out once or twice, and when the prospect is unresponsive, the salesperson will move on. This, despite research that states 20+ touches are often required to drive a single executive-level conversation! That's why it is critical to build those 20+ touchpoints into a system allowing salespeople to provide value and be persistent while not being seen as a pest.

With a closed pipeline that moves prospects from one campaign system to another in theoretically endless loops, we'll ensure a prospect continues to be *prospected* until a conversation is generated or they are pulled out of the pipeline.

In establishing campaign systems with our own clients, we find it helpful to ask what they've learned to keep top of mind – or what has gone wrong in the past – when:

Generating prospects?

Qualifying prospects as worthy of outreach?

Driving sales meetings?

In conversations with buyers?

During proposal issuance or acceptance to increase conversion?

In generating referrals?

In each of the above areas, what are things they've learned to *ensure they should avoid doing*?

Incorporating those answers as you build your outreach systems will ensure your campaigns accomplish their goal of getting prospects closer to the sale instead of repeating what's gone wrong in the past.

If your salespeople have been left to their own devices to manage and create their own pipelines and campaigns, you'll need to meet with them to create a standardized version of their outreach steps for your prospects' sales cycle. While you are welcome to adopt the names of the campaigns I've outlined here, you may also find they're called something different among your team or in your industry, and it's best to use your 'native tongue.' You may also find the model outlined here serves as a good foundation, but your sales cycle may involve purchase orders, delayed payment schedules, or any of the hundreds of permutations in the world of sales. Take those into account as you map out the overview of the campaign systems you'll ask salespeople to adopt.

Let's take the 'Cold Outreach Campaign' as an example and walk through how a campaign system looks during creation and rollout.

Establishing a Campaign System

Trigger: When establishing each vertical of a pipeline.

Bulletproof Impact: Defining specific outreach steps ensures salespeople maintain communication with prospects, allows them to schedule future outreach, and ensures salespeople make more than a two-call effort to engage prospects in conversation.

Overview: Explain that as part of the efforts to increase everyone's sales (and commissions), you'll be looking at capturing best practices for how to reach out to new prospects and generate sales conversations. As you're starting with the

51

first point of outreach on a new prospect, ask yourself/your team: "What have we noticed works well in qualifying prospects and getting them into initial sales conversations?"

You'll want to pay attention to a few areas that will begin to surface:

1. Methods

You'll quickly see if your team favors a certain medium when reaching out to new contacts (email, social media, phone, etc.). Pay attention to which method generates the best response from otherwise 'cold' or indifferent prospects.

If you're creating the campaign on your own, ask what methods of outreach generate your best initial conversations. Are you meeting your best prospects at networking events (in-person methods)? Are you having great initial conversations on the phone to set appointments (phone calls)? Is your best luck with conducting virtual sessions (social media/video)?

2. Messaging

Once you've captured the best methods to use in contacting new prospects, capture the messaging that your salespeople find works best for generating initial conversations. Across each communication method, map out what you or your team normally says, asks, or shares with their prospects that qualifies decision makers, determines budgets, and reveals buying timeframes. The end-product of this exercise will be the outline of emails, social media messages, direct mail templates, and outreach scripts.

If you're running a solo operation and mapping outreach methods on your own, it's a good idea to look back on past clients that *didn't* come in through warm referrals (i.e., the ones you developed on your own). Reconstruct the prospect's journey in becoming a client, tracking the mediums used. For instance, was an email followed by a LinkedIn message followed by a phone call that generated the sales meeting? If you don't have many sales under your belt or are standing up your first sales team, connect with your industry's sales veterans and fuel their coffee habit by buying a round in exchange for learning what works best in establishing rapport with new prospects.

3. Movement

What pieces of information do we need from a prospect to move an account out of the current vertical and into the next one? In this case, how do we move from the 'cold outreach' vertical into either the decision-maker identified (where we know who a decision maker is) or preselect (we know a decision maker, budget and buying window)? If you or your salespeople determine that finding the decision maker justifies moving a prospect into a new campaign system, now you have a *campaign goal* for your cold outreach campaign. Every outreach campaign, whatever you call it, should have a goal that, when achieved, moves a prospect out of that campaign and drops them into a more 'valuable' stage and campaign system in your pipeline.

Are We on the Same Sheet of Music?

Ensure that you don't leave your planning session without codifying at least the beta version of a cold outreach campaign system. The reason for this is that in order to create a Bulletproof sales system, salespeople have to be operating from the same sheet of music even if their key, notes, and pitch occasionally differ.

This beta version may look like a letter followed by a note card followed by a phone call followed by an email with a week's gap in between each step, each with a template that can then be edited and customized by your salespeople for each prospect.

Don't worry about your campaign systems being perfect out of the gate; more important is that what your team is doing is consistent, because that's the only way it can be systematically improved.

What might an initial campaign system and cadence look like once it's built? Each of your campaigns should be defined by their stage in your prospect's sales cycle, the type of outreach, cadence in between contact points, and associated templates/scripts. Mapped into a linear format, it might appear like this:

Campaign System: Cold Outreach

Step 1 (day of launch): Ensure contact data is accurate and that we have a phone number or email address for likely decision makers in the account. Send LinkedIn invite message using invitation template.

Step 2 (2 days in): Phone call. If voicemail is left, use voicemail script.

Step 3 (7 days in): Email. Use Cold Outreach email template #1 and customize to account decision maker.

Step 4 (14 days in): Phone call. If voicemail is left, use voicemail script.

Step 5 (20 days in): Send Cold Outreach letter to business mailing address on account. Use Cold Outreach letter template.

With a Bulletproof selling system comprised of a standardized pipeline, campaigns, cadences, templates, and scripts, a sales manager's role becomes more about managing, improving, and closing performance gaps than nudging salespeople to make more calls.

Systemizing Success with Campaign Systems

At this point, construct beta-versions of the campaign systems below, defining the methods of outreach and the name of any associated template (even if the template doesn't exist right now). We'll be creating and systemizing each element in coming chapters.

Cold Outreach

(They don't know much about us)

Step 1: Launch Date

Method of outreach = (Call, email, social media, direct mail, etc.)

Name of template or script, if one exists =

Step 2: X Days after initial launch
Method of outreach = (Call, email, social media, direct mail, etc.)
Name of template or script, if one exists =
Step 3: X Days after initial launch
Method of outreach = (Call, email, social media, direct mail, etc.)
Name of template or script, if one exists =
(Add additional steps as needed)

Decision-Maker Identified
(We know who the economic buyer in the account is)
Step 1: Launch Date
Method of outreach = (Call, email, social media, direct mail, etc.)
Name of template or script, if one exists =
Step 2: X Days after initial launch
Method of outreach = (Call, email, social media, direct mail, etc.)
Name of template or script, if one exists =
Step 3: X Days after initial launch
Method of outreach = (Call, email, social media, direct mail, etc.)
Name of template or script, if one exists =
(Add additional steps as needed)

Could Not Reach/No Response
(Previous campaign systems haven't generated a response)
Step 1: Launch Date
Method of outreach = (Call, email, social media, direct mail, etc.)
Name of template or script, if one exists =
Step 2: X Days after initial launch
Method of outreach = (Call, email, social media, direct mail, etc.)
Name of template or script, if one exists =
Step 3: X Days after initial launch

Method of outreach = (Call, email, social media, direct mail, etc.)

Name of template or script, if one exists =

(Add additional steps as needed)

Pre-Select

(We know who the economic buyer is, potential budget, and buying window)

Step 1: Launch Date

Method of outreach = (Call, email, social media, direct mail, etc.)

Name of template or script, if one exists =

Step 2: X Days after initial launch

Method of outreach = (Call, email, social media, direct mail, etc.)

Name of template or script, if one exists =

Step 3: X Days after initial launch

Method of outreach = (Call, email, social media, direct mail, etc.)

Name of template or script, if one exists =

(Add additional steps as needed)

With basic steps of each of your campaigns outlined and those campaign systems aligned with pipeline stages, you've done more to systemize your selling than most salespeople do in a career.

While many salespeople only have lagging indicators to judge success such as closed sales, having a campaign map like the one you created above provides the ability to quickly get a snapshot of sales performance in the following ways:

1. Use of Systems

It is easy for a sales manager to look into the CRM of any of their salespeople, especially in an enterprise-wide CRM, and ensure adherence to campaigns, cadences, and templates. If you find your salespeople's outreach tasks have become overdue, or call notes do not align with the campaign-generated task of 'Call the Prospect,' you'll know something is wrong long before a sale is in jeopardy. While no system is impossible for a salesperson to 'game,' the raw amount of work it takes to make a campaign system *look* like it's being used will discourage most salespeople from attempting to fabricate steps.

2. Account Progress

Because we encourage standing up multiple verticals/ campaigns that represent the stages of a sales cycle, sales managers can get a snapshot of any of their salespeople's complete pipelines at-a-glance and take appropriate action to aid their salespeople in moving stalled accounts in the proper direction. For instance, if one of your salespeople has more prospects in the 'cold outreach' stage than in the 'decision maker identified' stage of their pipeline, you can deliver training that helps that salesperson identify decision makers within their accounts.

3. Getting Orphaned Accounts 'Back on the Rails'

In even the best salesperson's pipeline, some accounts orphan through lack of a follow-up step. If these accounts are still qualified and worth pursuing, a sales manager has the ability with most CRMs to see which accounts haven't had contact in a while and can nudge them back into play for their salesperson by launching that account into a campaign system.

Now that we understand how to construct campaigns with our teams, it's important to assess what we've actually created that may have never existed in the history of our organization: An actual system for generating revenue that exists outside the heads of the top-performing salespeople.

When I coach military veterans returning to the workforce, I warn them that they've been trained to have the performance capability of a Porsche. Why is that a warning, and how does it apply to Bulletproof systems? If you take even a mid-sized sedan and push it further than it's capable of performing, you're asking for a crash. Ask my first car, a 1993 Ford Taurus that lasted two weeks in my care and wasn't made to corner mountain roads at 60 mph.

The danger in using any system designed for high performance is that it requires different handling. While we'll go over exactly how to do this with the input of your sales team, it's imperative to know that no continuously improving system, especially a Bulletproof one, is set-it-and-forget-it. Most systems our clients were or weren't using prior to learning about Bulletproof selling were just that. Those systems sometimes got the job done, but because they were rarely updated, it never allowed users to know what they were truly capable of achieving. When the environment a system is designed for changes and the system doesn't adapt, results quickly deteriorate. It's the law of entropy in effect within our pipeline.

One of the first symptoms of entropy occurs with lost prospects, so let's solve a problem that has plagued salespeople for as long as they've been pursuing prospects: ensure we never inadvertently lose touch with a prospect again.

CHAPTER 7

Eliminating Prospect Attrition

IF IT'S NOT glaringly obvious by this point, Bulletproof teams, whether in the military or on the battlefield of sales, take the initiative. While studying teams in combat environments, I noticed Marines were constantly looking for places where they could capture an advantage. What I never saw a Bulletproof team do, on the battlefield or in the boardroom, was *leave their success in someone else's court.* As I've worked with sales teams, I found this principle is not practiced regularly. Too many times I've seen salespeople hang up with a qualified decision maker who told them, "Send along your information and we'll call you if we're interested" or "fill out the request-for-proposal and our committee will let you know if they have questions." Then the salesperson simply did what they were told and waited for the prospect to call back.

I slap my own head when I see salespeople not applying the most powerful principle in selling: owning the next step.

Sealing Prospect Leaks System

Trigger: When developing campaign systems, ensure the three potential pipeline leaks are sealed to prevent prospect attrition.

Bulletproof Impact: Ensures you or your salespeople don't have to rely on any prospect to take action, reach back out, or respond in order to keep their account in play.

We advise our clients to systemize owning the next step by using campaign systems that generate tasks for salespeople to complete if prospects don't respond to previous outreach attempts. To ensure our CRM does the job of keeping prospects in play, we need to ensure that our pipelines are airtight.

Systemizing Success with the Sealing Prospect Leaks System: Ensuring Follow-Up Tasks Appear

How do we ensure we seal potential leaks and maintain initiative on any prospect's journey through our pipeline? Whenever a prospect is reached via phone or sits down for an in-person or virtual meeting, the first potential for a leak occurs.

Bulletproof salespeople ensure they control the next point of outreach after a conversation, not leaving it in the hands of the prospect.

That twenty-two-word sentence could fill the pages of its own book; that's how impactful it is to the success of salespeople. And it's required by every one of our clients' sales teams, whether they are running campaigns to drive meetings or spending all day interacting face-to-face with prospects. When a salesperson is managing prospects at scale, they can't be expected to remember that a single prospect was supposed to get back to them. For that reason, Bulletproof salespeople ensure there's a follow-up step on every prospect across their entire pipeline, even if that next step is a few months away.

Sealing this leak is as simple as entering a manual follow-up step on an account after a prospect interaction to ensure it comes back in front of a salesperson if a prospect doesn't respond. This alone will solve most prospect attrition.

The next two places 'leaks' can occur are within our CRMs and campaign systems, at the top and the bottom of each campaign's set of outreach tasks.

Systemizing Success with the Sealing Prospect Leaks System: Sealing the Top of Campaign Systems

Often, a salesperson will want to launch a new campaign on a prospect because they discovered a decision maker within a key account. However, sometimes that buyer isn't returning to the office for another two weeks, is at a conference, or is otherwise unavailable. The prospect is at the beginning of that campaign system's outreach steps but is not ready for the salesperson to conduct outreach. Too many salespeople will let a deal stall at this point, hoping they remember to reach back out to their prospect and restart the campaign system when the prospect is back in the office.

The untold billions of dollars of lost revenue from that one error is enough to buy a few Caribbean islands, as it orphans the account from future contact. Unless a savvy sales manager regularly checks through their sales teams' deals for orphan accounts, it could be years before these types of account come back in front of the salesperson, if ever. However, because we're using a CRM to manage our prospects, a salesperson can hold off launching the full campaign system they'd use if contact would be possible today and create a manual task on that account with a simple statement such as, "Launch decision maker campaign on X date." From there, the salesperson can assign that manual task a date to get it back in front of them when the decision maker *will* be back in the office.

Systemizing Success with the Sealing Prospect Leaks System: Sealing the Bottom of Campaign Systems

Even if we've shored up the potential leak that may occur when we move an account into a new campaign but need to delay outreach, there is another leak that often happens at the other end of a campaign's outreach steps – when all the steps in the campaign have been executed but the objectives that move the account forward haven't been achieved. If an account flows all the way through your outreach steps and is unresponsive, it should move to a lower-value pipeline vertical and into a campaign designed to re-engage that prospect. Unless your CRM has the ability to automate movement of an account between verticals in your pipeline, movement from one campaign to another is a manual task that must be accomplished by salespeople.

We've found the best way to seal leaks that occur at the bottom of campaigns is to have the last task of the campaign specifically tell a salesperson to move the account to another vertical and launch that vertical's associated outreach campaign. This could look like a final campaign step of: "If prospect account is unresponsive, move to XYZ vertical and launch that vertical's campaign."

Ninety-nine percent of the time, that task handles the account movement and prevents orphans as the salesperson sees the task appear in their 'to-do list' or dashboard and executes it. Many accounts benefit from a rest between cadence cycles, so there may be a time delay from one account's end to another's launch. It's here some salespeople hope they remember to launch a new campaign on an account in the future, and again, untold revenue can be lost. To prevent this, we encourage salespeople to create a second follow-up task on the account to 'ensure XYZ campaign has launched on Bob at X date' and assign the task a date so the account comes back in front of the salesperson as a contingency. It might seem redundant, but with a manually created task, even if the CRM software drops the ball on firing the next campaign system, the account will still come in front of the salesperson again for pursuit.

While this chapter is heavy with CRM-related language, the key takeaway is to ensure all qualified prospects remain in play. To do that, salespeople can't *hope* to remember to follow up. That function should be owned by your salespeople after every prospect interaction and can be systemized within our CRMs.

If you've gone as far as defining deal stages and mapping out campaign systems, you've created a Porsche-style sales vehicle. And like any high-performing vehicle, bad fuel will ensure it never performs as well as it could, and in some cases, guarantee it never performs at all.

For that reason, we've devoted the next chapter to the fuel that runs your Bulletproof sales engine – your prospects.

CHAPTER 8

Fueling Your Bulletproof Pipeline

WHEN MILITARY TEAMS look back on the time they spend conducting missions, it easily factors to 80% or more of their time engaged in research, prep, and planning, with 20% or less engaged in executing the mission. Why do they spend so much time preparing, planning, and conducting dry runs?

They've learned an important lesson: "The more we prepare, the less we bleed."

While that would be a macabre analogy to apply with a sales team, salespeople will understand that, "The more we prepare for making the sale, the less sales we'll lose." That comes from the training and systems we give to our salespeople *and* the quality of the prospects they pursue.

Prioritizing Prospects System

Trigger: When it's time to load existing prospects into your Bulletproof pipeline and whenever sourcing new prospects for outreach.

Bulletproof Impact: Ensuring only the highest-quality leads appear in your salespeople's pipelines drastically improves closing ratios as priority is given to accounts with a history or high likelihood of purchasing your product or service.

After tracking the results of more than 8,000 sales calls in my own company, we've discovered that we can largely determine the future success of a sale by the research we conduct on our prospects before making the first contact.

To clarify: It's possible to know how likely a prospect is to buy what we're selling before we ever have a conversation with them and, by using the systems described in this book, unseat an incumbent provider.

The first thing we must do is to get clear on who our product or service *isn't* a right fit for. That way we can eliminate a fair swath of the billions of people on the planet and further cull through those who remain to define our ideal sets of clients. Whenever we look at the prospect list of our clients' salespeople, it's not hard to see that many of those prospects will never buy from them. How do we know if a prospect *is* viable and worth the omni-channel pursuit that converts prospects?

Across thousands of prospects and hundreds of industries, the first filter we've found that will determine someone's likelihood of becoming a customer is: Have they bought our product or service, or something like it, in the past?

If a prospect has a history of purchasing what your salespeople offer, there's an astronomically higher probability they'll purchase something like it again, should the need arise. This especially applies to high-cost, intangible services like coaching, consulting, and training. Trying to convince someone who's never purchased what you offer isn't impossible, but it's a much harder hill to climb.

What if you're going to market with an innovative solution that no one's purchased yet, because it simply hasn't been available? Ask: Who's purchased something *like* this? Knowing that ahead of time will allow your salespeople to more easily build a bridge between your product and something prospects are familiar with.

Once you have an industry or group of prospects who meet the criteria of having purchased something like what you're offering in the past, the next determinant in a high-quality prospect list is the prospect's annual revenue, especially if it will limit their ability to purchase your product or service. That can often be determined by the size of the company and/or where it is located.

Next, consider the prospect's geography if you're limited to selling in certain regions, states, nations, hemispheres, etc. Or perhaps you only sell to people in a certain set of industries. That means when standing up Bulletproof systems, all other industries can be left out of your pipelines.

Once there is a list of high-quality potentials that meet the minimum criteria above, the next step is prioritizing them for outreach. Avoid dumping everyone into a pipeline's campaign systems at once. While everyone on the initial list *could* purchase what you're selling if budget and need coincided at the moment you get in touch with them, there will be a tier of high-value prospects who:

- Have a history of purchasing what you're selling
- Are likely connected formally or informally to someone who has purchased from you in the past
- Have a regular/recurring need for what you sell
- Know they need your product or service, although they may not know your company has the ability to provide it
- Have identifiable decision makers or people with fiduciary power, usually identified by job title
- Are in the regions, states, nations, or hemispheres you can sell or deliver to
- Have contact information for outreach that you can obtain

This initial list allows salespeople to qualify who they should be reaching out to first. Prospects that have all these attributes are what we consider 'qualified' prospects, although some research is always required to fill in a solid contact profile. If a prospect has most of the above attributes but is missing one, they fall to the next tier in priority. If two pieces of data are missing, they fall to the third tier, etc. This will allow sales leaders sourcing leads for their salespeople to accomplish a few important things:

1. Equitably parse leads to your salespeople if you, a lead-generating service, or your marketing team are providing leads.
2. Inspire your salespeople to put more effort into outreach as they know they are pursuing highly qualified leads.
3. Greatly increase closing ratios and pipeline conversion.
4. Coach salespeople through consistent sales systems as their leads will all be *capable* of buying, even if they aren't willing to buy from you or your company right now.

Of course, providing or assisting salespeople in generating qualified leads is not meant to dissuade them from generating their own prospects. Rather, it is designed to give them model prospects to pursue and parameters to use when discovering their own high-quality leads.

Systemizing Success with Prioritizing Prospects

What information should you ensure is researched and input into your CRM for each prospect *before* salespeople make initial contact with a campaign system?

- Name and direct contact information of the executive director or CEO of the organization. The information of a company's leader becomes helpful if your team needs to 'unstick' an account that's become unresponsive.
- Name and direct contact information of the likely decision maker in the organization if they're different from the CEO.
- Mailing address for direct mail and handwritten cards.
- Websites for the organization, staff contact info, and dates of any events that are tied to your product or service's use.
- Past vendors or suppliers of our product or service to that organization so we can differentiate ourselves with our unique value and have a strong call premise.

"But what about things like budget, decision-making process, or buying windows?" you may be asking. "Don't you want to know those things as well?"

Absolutely, but unless an organization is required to publish that information on a public-facing website, it's almost impossible to find without speaking to a human within the prospect's company. Critical data points such as budget, decision-making process, or buying windows form the backbone of the discovery questions we'll build scripts around in an upcoming chapter.

After gathering initial information on prospects, we next need to define what pieces of information, if we had them, would drastically increase our salespeople's ability to sell. Those questions will seed our future calling scripts and communication templates. It shouldn't be a surprise that there's a system for that, too.

Prospect Intelligence Profile System

Trigger: When sourcing new prospects and when developing discovery questions for scripts.

Bulletproof Impact: By defining what additional pieces of data would make your salespeople's jobs easier, you can task salespeople or researchers to comb through any publicly available websites or databases to gather critical information before initial outreach. If that information isn't publicly available, the remaining questions form the backbone of discovery questions salespeople can ask to build exceptional prospect profiles and aid in future conversion.

As you examine your top-tier prospects for what data might be missing from their accounts, ask what pieces of information, if you *did* have them, would make selling smoother?

Don't limit yourself to what's available online or on LinkedIn – really shoot for the stars.

Systemizing Success with Prospect Intelligence Profiles

There's a reason games played on the home field put the home team at an advantage; home teams know the terrain, even if dealing with a new opponent. If you could access it, would any of the following help you or your salespeople?:

- Name of likely decision maker in the prospect company
- That decision maker's contact information, including direct phone numbers, email address, LinkedIn profile URL, and any other social media channels they frequent
- Mailing address for sending direct mail
- Any challenges they or their employees or clients are facing right now that your product or service could be a solution for
- Companies or individuals they used in the past for the product or service you're offering or a similar product/service
- The budget they likely paid for your product or service from a past provider
- What their likely budget is for their next round of purchasing your product or service
- When/what time of year they are likely to be purchasing the product or service you offer
- If the product or service you offer is designed to be used at a specific time (for a meeting or event, for instance), when that meeting or event is supposed to occur
- How many people in and outside your prospect's company your product or service could benefit
- How many sites or locations in their company could use your product or service
- The names of likely decision makers in those other divisions or areas where you may be able to sell additional products or services within the same company
- The names and contact information of any other decision makers in other companies the prospect may be connected with

The list could go on for dozens of additional items and will likely be unique to the product or service you offer, so take the time to map out the data that would make it easier to make contact with your prospects and sell your product or service. The secondary value in mapping out all of these things is that it will build powerful discovery questions to ask when making contact with prospects. Once these discovery questions are built into call scripts (a system we'll dive into in-depth), your CRM can be formatted to have these critical data points show up as the first fields a salesperson sees in each prospect's profile.

Now that you have ways to identify quality leads for yourself and your salespeople to pursue, as well as a list of critical data points to research or discover during outreach and outreach campaigns to get your salespeople in front of those prospects, it's time to fire the ignition up on the high-performance sales vehicle you've built. In the next chapter, we'll show you how to systemize success with every outreach attempt your salespeople make whether a sale is made or not.

CHAPTER 9

Systemizing Success With Prospect Interactions

MANY SALESPEOPLE CONDUCT a lot of activity over the course of a given day, week, and sometimes even a month but have almost no pipeline movement to show for it. This means a lot of calls made and emails sent to the same accounts without getting one step closer to the sale, even if they are talking to a person who can say 'Yes'!

David Allen, one of the most prolific time-management trainers in the world, is famous for saying, "You can do anything, but not everything." Too many salespeople are attempting to accomplish all their goals with every prospect conversation. For prospects that convert on a single call or meeting, that's great – but few do.

Salespeople are often under the assumption that they must accomplish everything on a single call, which is one of the chief causes of call reluctance.

Instead of turning on the Bulletproof sales vehicle you've built and simply asking salespeople to sell more, we've seen the best results from our clients when clear objectives are provided that are achievable with every prospect interaction.

The Micro-Objective System
Trigger: When establishing campaign systems and call scripts.

Bulletproof Impact: For many salespeople, not making a sale on every call can be demoralizing even if they sell a high-cost item in an industry with a long sales cycle. This comes from not understanding the data that must be in place before they can be ideally positioned to ask for the prospect's business. Gathering that data can serve as micro-objectives for salespeople to strive for in every prospect exchange, allowing them to change their definition of success from 'selling something' to 'being better positioned for a future sale than we were yesterday.'

For the teams I embedded with around the world, their work was dangerous, demanding, and done in rapidly changing environments. Each mission always had a primary objective such as 'clear these four city blocks,' just as our salespeople are told, 'meet this minimum sales goal.' However, there are also 'even better if' goals Bulletproof teams are asked to pursue on every mission. These could include such items as bringing back high-value prisoners, gathering additional intelligence to help other teams in the area, and of course bringing everyone back alive.

Bulletproof teams have minimum/maximum objectives to pursue; not just one benchmark for success, but many. And of course, the more objectives a team can achieve on a single mission, the better off their organizations will be.

Let's contrast that with the way most salespeople are taught to set goals for calls and scheduling sales meetings. Some organizations give their salespeople training, leads, and a sales quota, then tell them 'go out there and sell' and wonder why turnover and lagging results are an issue! Few organizations give their salespeople objectives for each client contact such that even if a sale isn't made, measurable progress occurs toward an eventual sale.

Instead of complicating sales, these types of micro-objectives allow salespeople to have verifiable proof of progress while also creating forward movement in their pipelines. As a sales manager myself, it's imperative for me to know that if every prospect contact doesn't generate a sale, it should at least get the account closer to one in the future. Simply hearing a salesperson report, "The prospect isn't buying now," tells me nothing about the account's value, decision makers, decision-making process, etc. Basically, that statement means we know nothing more than we did before we made the call or stopped by the prospect's office!

While your organization's micro-objectives will differ depending on your industry, customer buying cycle, budget, etc., there are *always* things your salespeople can leave a prospect conversation with that will prepare that account for a successful conversion in the future.

This is where Bulletproof selling systems come in, specifically the separate deal stages that make up the verticals in your pipeline. Micro-objectives are the trigger mechanisms that move an account from one campaign system in your pipeline to another even if a sale doesn't occur.

For instance, if we call on a prospect we know very little about, the salesperson has an opportunity to discover who makes buying decisions in that organization for our product or service, specific challenges they're suffering from that our product or service alleviates, how the company makes decisions to purchase, when they make those decisions and at what budget ranges. That's five micro-objectives a salesperson can leave a call having achieved even if the prospect didn't purchase today. Having that data easily accessible in a CRM will make any future sale in that account much smoother. When a salesperson checks what campaign system a prospect is in, they'll know what deal stage they're trying to move a prospect into next. That will reveal exactly what secondary or tertiary objectives they'll need to pursue in their next outreach to move the account forward and consider that interaction a success.

Systemizing Success with Micro-Objectives

Below are the series of data points we advise our clients use to form their outreach objectives, but you may have others that are required to ensure your product fits in the prospect's floorspace, maintains compliance with local and state regulations, does not conflict with client policies, etc. In other words, modify your micro-objectives depending on your unique product or service's customer requirements.

To train your salespeople in their use, roleplay with a sales leader acting as a prospect. We make a game out of this with our clients' new salespeople and encourage bonuses on the sales calls where salespeople capture all their micro-objectives, even if a sale isn't made. The more questions salespeople can ask and get answers to, the closer they are to being able to position your product or service as an ideal solution when a prospect *is* in a buying window or capable of purchasing.

Objective 1. Identify the Decision Maker

Many people in an organization have the ability to say no, but few can say yes. The more expensive or wide-reaching your product or service is, the fewer people there are who can say 'yes.' In order to maximize your time and your salespeople's time, it's vital the decision maker(s) for what you sell are quickly identified and/or updated within your CRM. Confirming a decision maker – or reconfirming one from a legacy account – is an awesome micro-objective for any outreach attempt.

Objective 2. Confirm Need

Few people care about the product or service you sell. They *do* care about the problems they're suffering from or growth they want to achieve. In order to earn the right to offer your product or service as a solution to their problem, confirm a need actually exists. Asking for and capturing needs and challenges from a decision maker or even a gatekeeper within an account is a micro-objective that will serve a salesperson well in later conversations.

Objective 3. Confirm the Impact of the Prospect's Challenges

While this could be considered objective 2.5, it's valuable enough to stand alone. In order to justify the cost of your product or service, *especially* a service, you need to know what the ROI is likely to be for your prospect. If it's impossible to determine the exact financial impact of your product or service because much of it depends on client implementation, then you can at least determine how many individuals your product or service will touch and calculate potential impact to $X dollars of payroll, $X dollars of lost revenue if nothing changes, etc.

Objective 4. Confirm Buying Timeframe

In many organizations, there will be cases where bureaucracy or a budgetary cycle or a contract renewal period prevents some products or services from being purchased at the moment your salesperson is in a conversation with the decision maker. In that case, a micro-objective can be to confirm a follow-up date with that decision maker and schedule a meeting when they will be empowered to make a buying decision.

Objective 5. Qualify for Budget

Why is this question not earlier in the list? It's a moot point to discuss a $5 million-dollar widget if a decision maker doesn't know they have a $200 million-dollar problem the widget can solve. Additionally, budgets sometimes change for decision makers between now and whenever they *can* make a buying decision, just as our fees may change from one year to the next. This is why confirming potential budget or budget range is a micro-objective always worth pursuing *after* needs have been identified or reconfirmed.

6. Examine Other Opportunities Within the Organization

While you or your salesperson may be speaking with the *main* decision maker, it doesn't mean they're the only one with fiduciary power in the company. This applies for both business-to-business and business-to-consumer sales. A great micro-objective is also discovering any other divisions, offices, events, or branches of that company that might also be suffering from that need or desire those improved outcomes your product or service provides.

7. Examine Opportunities Outside the Organization

We *do* advise this question be saved until the end of the conversation, as it's used to generate external referrals. While many salespeople are uncomfortable asking for a referral before their product or service has even been sold or delivered, sales experts from Zig Ziglar to Grant Cardone advocate asking for referrals from prospects early and often. A salesperson who doesn't leave a call with a sale but does leave with qualified leads can absolutely consider that call a success – making this a micro-objective worth pursuing.

If your salespeople create questions that elicit those answers and actually ask those questions when in conversations with decision makers, here's what they'll be able to accomplish that they may not have been doing before:

- Confirmed who in the account should be contacted via email, phone, LinkedIn, carrier pigeon, etc.
- Fleshed out *exactly* what that organization's or individual's challenges and growth goals are that can be used as future call premises and research points to continue to add value
- Quantified the impact of your product or service for their organization (this will be specific to each buyer, even if there are multiple decision makers within a single account)
- Confirmed when the buyer would be willing to buy, allowing your salesperson to project potential revenue in their pipeline, often down to the month or week
- Confirmed this buyer has the budget to invest in the product or service, avoiding the ever-present 'unqualified account' that stalls most salespeople's pipelines
- Identify other buyers within the organization to add to the salesperson's pipeline and begin pursuit with

- Generated at least a few referrals to scrub and get into play

Sales managers would be overjoyed if every conversation with a decision maker yielded half of those above results – but *all of them? For* every *conversation with a decision maker?* Even the top salespeople in the top sales teams on the planet rarely produce results that consistent, so it's easy to imagine the impact it would make if every salesperson on a team was able to leave each conversation with that much actionable intelligence, even if the sale couldn't be made that day to that prospect.

If you're a solopreneur/entrepreneur, striving for micro-objectives in every sales conversation will easily put you into the top 1% of entrepreneurs on the planet and ensure you are pursuing quality prospects that are generating revenue sooner, paying what your product and service is worth, and generating new prospects for you to pursue.

How do we define what micro-objectives our salespeople should be pursuing on each call? Let's go through the different deal stages or verticals of a pipeline and outline what micro-objectives are possible even if a sale isn't made. Again, your sales cycle may have more or less steps so feel free to add to or subtract from these stages based on what you and your sales team have identified as the stages of your prospects' buying journey.

Cold Outreach Stage:

Definition of this stage: The prospect is unfamiliar with us and/or most of their leadership team has transitioned since our last contact.

What we should walk into the conversation with: Names of likely decision makers, direct phone numbers and emails if they can be found online, LinkedIn profile URLs.

Primary objective: Make the sale.

Micro-objectives for prospects in this stage: Confirm the name and contact information of the person responsible for buying your product or service. Discover challenges they're experiencing that your product or service could alleviate. Discover budget. Discover buying process (single person, committee, what they need to review, etc.). Discover buying timeline. Set next meeting.

Decision Maker Known Stage:

Definition of this stage: We know the decision maker's name and likely their direct contact information, but may not know the specific challenges they're experiencing, what budget they have for our product or service, or what their buying process or timeline might be.

What we should walk into the conversation with: Name of the decision maker and their contact information.

Primary objective: Make the sale.

Micro-objectives for prospects in this stage: Discover challenges our product or service could help alleviate. Discover personal goals of decision maker as it applies to the solutions our product or service provides. Discover budget. Discover buying process (single person, committee, etc.). Discover buying timeline. Discover number of people affected by their challenges. Find out if there are any additional buyers within other departments of their organization. Set next meeting.

Pre-Select Stage:

Definition: We know who the decision maker is, we're in the timeframe they said they'll be buying in, and we know their potential budget justifies further conversation.

What we should walk into the conversation with: Decision maker contact information, notes from previous chats. Budget range. Buying process (single person, committee, etc.)

Primary objective: Make the sale.

Micro-objectives for prospects in this stage: Confirm latest challenges and what they're looking for in our type of product or service before purchasing. Re-confirming buying process is a great one to get at this point as well (single person, a committee, what they need to review, etc.), as the prospect is close to purchasing and may have changed the buying process since last contact. As these accounts are in active selection mode, if they're not ready for a proposal or invoice, then another goal is to assess what the prospect still needs to see or receive to be ready for a proposal or invoice. Set firm follow-up appointment.

Could Not Reach Stage:

Definition: The results of our outreach attempts in another campaign system were not responded to. We target this vertical of our campaign to the executive director or CEO if possible as we weren't able to get traction with a lower-level decision maker.

What we should walk into the conversation with: The name of the decision maker and their contact information AND the executive director or CEO's name, as well as their contact information (this is the decision maker's boss if they're not the CEO themselves).

Primary objective: Make the sale.

Micro-objectives for prospects in this stage: To have a conversation with the executive director or CEO to confirm whether the decision maker you have still works there and if they're still the ones responsible for deciding about purchasing your product or service. Discover the executive director or CEO's ideal outcomes that your product or service could play a role in delivering. Get their permission to CC them in an email to the decision maker to restart the conversation about setting an appointment with you or the salesperson. An executive or mid-level manager getting a message from their boss saying 'have a conversation with these folks' is a great way to restart a stalled deal with someone who wouldn't respond otherwise.

To scale our sales efforts, progress is not always measured by today's actualized revenue. Rather, progress is defined by being better prepared than anyone else to do business with that account when they are purchasing what we sell.

For a Bulletproof sales team, *every* interaction with a prospect should result in forward account movement.

Notice that we are attempting to 'fill in' any missing details of our prospects' information with every outreach attempt, regardless of their buying stage in our pipeline. While a phone call can often move a prospect from one end of the pipeline (we know very little) to the other end of the pipeline (we have all we need to issue a proposal or invoice) in a few minutes, moving towards those micro-objectives can be achieved through questions built into every email, LinkedIn message, voicemail, and direct mail letter.

Next, let's focus on systemizing those individual templates and scripts to ensure that every time we communicate with a prospect, we're being seen as professionals willing to take the time to serve prospects with customized value.

CHAPTER 10

Systemizing Templates And Scripts

SOMETHING AN OBSERVER will immediately notice while studying Bulletproof teams in action is that, while they are able to dynamically innovate when situations change, their level of performance remains high. In fact, if there is anything that separates a Bulletproof team from a non-Bulletproof one – in sales or in combat – it's their ability to maintain standards of excellence.

Whether it's engaging a prospect on the phone or clearing a building, Bulletproof teams perform consistently better than their peers because they don't have to fall back on 'winging it' or hoping they say or do the right things in front of prospects and clients.

What are the systems Bulletproof salespeople rely on to complete their everyday sales tasks? They would have to be something that can be relied on regardless of individual energy level or caffeine intake and be updated as folks learn something that improves their chances of success.

Fortunately, there are systems like those available and Bulletproof salespeople utilize them with every point of outreach: Call scripts and message templates.

While we've covered qualifying prospects and maintaining consistency of outreach with predetermined campaign sequences and omni-channel outreach, what is it that ensures we're using best practices when our salespeople interact with a prospect?

Like a team of Marines who have practiced the movements of clearing a house enough times to be able to unconsciously operate in that environment, call scripts and message templates allow salespeople to take the guesswork out of the most important part of their jobs: contacting people who need the value their product or service provides.

Many sales stall or fail because sales leaders *hope* their salespeople are customizing their messaging and that it's being communicated well.

Anyone with a LinkedIn account is aware that customized, value-added messaging is desperately lacking today. In the world of sales communication, it looks like a poorly written email, social media message, or fumbling phone conversation. If you take the time – along with the input of your team – to craft call scripts and messages templates as part of the campaign systems you've designed, you'll overcome most of the initial reluctance prospects might have in speaking with your salespeople while simultaneously taking hope out of your outreach strategy.

The Customized Messaging System

Trigger: When establishing message templates for email, social media and direct mail for each campaign system.

Bulletproof Impact: Instead of dealing with the fallout of poorly written emails salespeople invent on their own, rife with grammatical and formatting errors, templating messages within campaigns allow us to maintain a logical communication flow that tells the story we want our prospects to hear while incorporating best practices in moving from asynchronous communication (one-way) to the synchronous communication (two-way) that drives sales.

In the sales campaigns we've created for our clients, email, social media, and even direct mail play a vital role in getting the attention of prospects. Instead of hoping an email,

LinkedIn message, or letter will be so well-written it drives a return call, we advocate using all forms of asynchronous communication to build more certainty into getting a prospect's attention.

In Bulletproof teams, few things are done randomly, and messaging is the same in Bulletproof selling. Every message sent as part of a campaign system by your salespeople – and even messages sent outside a campaign – can achieve the impact they're there to deliver: driving a sales conversation.

We advocate the use of CRMs for our clients for a variety of reasons, not the least of which is the ability to program outreach tasks to occur in between phone calls.

When tasks to send messages *do* appear, CRMs also allow salespeople to quickly select pre-loaded message templates that correspond with a given campaign system. The salesperson can then quickly access the template in an email, customize the message to the prospect, and send them from within the CRM. Additionally, because a prospect is being managed in a specific campaign that corresponds with where they are in their buying journey, when a task to 'send email' appears as part of a campaign, salespeople can quickly identify and select the email, social media, or direct mail template for *that* task in *that* part of *that* campaign, customize the necessary portions, check for any errors, and hit 'send,' moving on to the next prospect's task for that day.

Systemizing Success with Customized Messaging

If you're designing message templates for your team, examine the overall pipeline you've created of your prospect's buying cycle and the corresponding campaigns. Phone calls and site visits should make up more than half of your outreach steps, so break up the remaining contact points across messaging channels: email, social media, direct mail, etc. For each contact point, determine what that particular message should contain so it flows logically from the previous campaign system step whether that was a phone call, email, social media message, letter, etc.

Name each message template so it corresponds with the task within the campaign. For example: Decision-Maker Identified Campaign Email #1.

When your salesperson sees the step of 'Send Decision Maker Identified Campaign Email #1,' they'll be able to quickly locate that template from within your CRM and load it for sending to the prospect.

In addition to being easy to find, messaging templates should also be easy to customize. The worst thing a system can do is produce more broken stuff, which is why salespeople should never use templated messages as a way to send even more generic, spammy 'Here's why we're awesome and why you should buy from us. Also, here's the link on my wide-open calendar to book some time with me so I can pitch you' messages.

To ensure messages are received and actually read, we'll need to customize them so they look like they were individually created for the prospect they're being sent to. By making the parts of a message template where customizations should occur easy to identify, salespeople can quickly scan for the pertinent information needed to replace template language and customize each message template they send.

While the art and craft of writing a good email, social media message, or direct mail letter is beyond the scope of this book, you can gather best practices from other books or from your own salespeople. The one thing we've found will ensure success regardless of a message's medium is to add value to your prospect with the message.

Here's an example of a template message within one of our clients' CRMs, with the actions the salesperson takes to customize the message in italics:

Decision Maker Identified Email #1

Salesperson is conducting their 'send message' tasks after completing phone calls that morning and sees their campaign system has triggered 'Decision Maker Identified Email #1' to be sent that day on Jim Smith's account. The salesperson opens Jim's account and selects Jim's email address. The CRM opens an email window with a drop-down of preloaded email templates. The salesperson selects 'Decision Maker Identified Email #1' from the list, which loads the template subject line and email body into the email window. In its raw form, it might look like this to the salesperson:

Subject: {{JOB TITLE}} - The Toughest Job on the Planet
{{First Name}}-

It only takes following a {{JOB TITLE}} around for one day to know it's the toughest job in any organization.

The clients we've had the pleasure of working with in {{GEOGRAPHY/REGION}} are telling us the {{INDUSTRY CHALLENGE}} has made their jobs more stressful than ever.

That's why we've decided to create a different type of service, one that partners with {{JOB TITLE}} to help {{BENEFIT 1}}, {{BENEFIT 2}}, and even {{BENEFIT 3}}.

I don't know if that kind of experience is what you're trying to create at {{PROSPECT COMPANY}}, so why don't we schedule a short call to help us learn more about what you're planning in the upcoming quarter? From there we can decide if it makes sense to discuss further.

Does this week work better for that or next?

The salesperson quickly scans the account information in Jim Smith's CRM records for the customization fields, sees that Jim is a distribution manager, and checks the new message for any grammatical or spelling errors before sending:

Subject: Distribution Manager - The Toughest Job on the Planet
Jim-

It only takes following a distribution manager around for one day to know it's the toughest job in any organization.

The clients we've had the pleasure of working with in the southeast distribution industry are telling us the changes in supply chain technology and evolving customer expectations have made their jobs more stressful than ever.

That's why we've decided to create a different type of service, one that partners with distribution managers to help ensure less errors in warehouse packaging, more on-time delivery, and even exceeding client expectations with value-added services.

I don't know if that kind of experience is what you're trying to create at Widget Distribution Company, so why don't we schedule a short call to help us learn more about what you're planning in the upcoming quarter? From there we can decide if it makes sense to discuss further.

Does this week work better for that or next?

Seeing no errors, salesperson hits 'send,' the email is sent from the salesperson's business email address linked within the CRM, and the salesperson checks the 'Send Decision Maker Identified Email #1' as being done on that account before moving on to the next messaging task in another prospect's account.

The total amount of time required for sending the above message – even allowing for customizations – is less than one minute. Not only did the salesperson not have to write the message from scratch, it is also highly customized to the prospect's details and incorporates best practices from the salesperson's marketing department and sales team for clear, concise, professional writing.

If there was a way to excise hope as a strategy in email communication with prospects, you've just been certified as an exorcist.

While asynchronous messaging can be systemized and automated across campaigns and outreach platforms, the best any system can do for systemizing *synchronous* communication such as phone calls is to generate a task: 'On this date, make phone call.' It's there that hope enters so many salespeople's worlds. However, by incorporating the type of training that Bulletproof teams undergo, we can prepare our salespeople for synchronous communication with prospects. This is the exact type of communication that quickly uncovers needs, qualifies buyers and budget, overcomes objections, and drives sales.

The Bulletproof Phone Script System

Trigger: When preparing salespeople to make initial calls to cold prospects.

Bulletproof Impact: Having a shared script available to all salespeople across geographies that addresses best practices in getting a prospect's attention and navigating commonly heard objections. Using a shared digital document also ensures that when an improvement is made or a salesperson discovers a new objection, it can be captured for the rest of the team's benefit.

Unfortunately, most salespeople approach sales calls the same way they would approach a personal call. They may know the name of the prospect they're calling, but not much else. Many salespeople assume they'll just call to 'check in' and see what happens. That would be akin to a group of Marines knowing a building was occupied by enemy combatants and wandering through the front door shouting, "Is anyone home?"

While prospects aren't our opponents, even junior salespeople have dealt with prospects that felt like combatants. Winging those interactions is not a recipe for success, for Marines on the battlefield or for Bulletproof salespeople.

That's where call scripts come in. Like any tool, call scripts can accelerate progress or do damage. Damage occurs when a salesperson recites from the script during calls. Accelerating progress occurs when a salesperson utilizes the script as a roadmap. The type of call scripts we've guided clients in creating – using a system we share below – are three-dimensional maps for navigating the terrain of prospect outreach.

In the 21st century, there's no excuse for anyone to print out a sales script and shuffle through its pages on a call. Unless your entire outreach script, discovery questions, and commonly heard objections can fit onto one sheet of paper, you'll need more than one page in your script, which is why we advocate digitizing them into an online word document.

Systemizing Success with Bulletproof Phone Scripts

The best call scripts have two levels we'll cover below: the first is the initial call flow to use in the opening seconds of the call, and the second level is systemizing responses to objections that guide prospects to the next step, whether that is a follow-on meeting with stakeholders or a sales conversation.

Here's a simple template to use to build a call script for yourself and your team that mirrors the order of the micro-objectives outlined earlier:

Initial Call Flow

Goal: May be *Identifying a Decision Maker* or *Information Gathering* or *Budget Qualifying*

Step 1: Identify decision maker

Ways of asking:

- Who's responsible for making decisions around ...
- Just wondering who's in charge of ...
- Not sure if you're the right person, I was just trying to find out who was responsible for ...

Step 2: Assess Challenges (when you're speaking with a decision maker)

- Great, I was wondering what you were looking to accomplish with ...
- Awesome, I'm calling because I read XYZ about your company on (website/publication) ...
- I saw that you were planning for X initiative, and I was wondering if the issues of ABC have come up as a concern ...

From Step 2, you and your salespeople can discover the things you need to know about your prospect to ascertain what type of product or service you offer that may be a good fit. We've devoted a whole chapter to what happens in a systemized sales conversation, so we'll remain focused on the initial conversation for now because it's in these initial discovery questions where Bulletproof salespeople will spend much of their call time as they further qualify prospects in their pipelines. It's what happens when a salesperson makes an ask for more time, a meeting, or consideration of purchasing that hope so often enters as a strategy. To replace hope with certainty, we'll need to prepare for the objections we're most likely to hear and ensure they are included in the same digital call script we've just created.

The Objection Response System

Trigger: When a prospect objects to the next step of the sales process.

Bulletproof Impact: Instead of salespeople having to learn how to overcome objections through hearing them from prospects – inevitably delaying that account's progress – objection scripts can ensure salespeople are bringing best practices to bear against prospect objections.

In every salesperson's memory are all the things they've ever been told that shut down a sales call or prevented a sale from moving forward. Salespeople hope they remember what they said that worked in the past to overcome a particular objection but rarely systemize great responses. To create an objection script, it's important to survey your team for the top dozen objections they've heard around your products or services. If your salespeople have worked out good responses, get those into your objection script as well.

Here are a few universal objections you and your salespeople should have responses for that can serve as jumping-off points for other objections that may be specific to your prospects:

- It's too expensive

- This is a bad time
- I don't know/like/trust you
- We have a legacy supplier that we're happy with
- We're still under contract with an existing supplier
- We won't be looking at making that buying decision until X date in the future
- I've had poor experiences with your product or service or brand in the past

With a little surveying, you'll likely uncover more objections that you and your salespeople have encountered. A good call script should be a searchable document, which is why we advocate they not live on paper. As your salespeople get used to working with the responses, they can use the search function available in digital documents to immediately search through dozens of pages of scripts and objections to get to the exact objection they're hearing, along with a suggested response flow.

A bonus to a shared digital script is that when the team discovers a better response to any particular objection, *everyone's* script can be updated with a few clicks. The next time salespeople pull up the document, it will be the latest version.

Systemizing Success with the Objection Response System

Objection scripts should be easily searchable. For instance, the objection for 'not enough money' should start with that exact wording – or something intuitively similar – so it is searchable by a salesperson. Next is the script they can use. The 'not enough money' objections look like this in many of our clients' digital scripts:

We can't afford anything or are not paying for (service) this year.

"Of course you don't have a big budget, money is tight everywhere these days. If we could work with you to reduce the overall fee, and even show you exactly how this will generate revenue so our product or service actually **makes you money** -

would that be of interest? Tell you what, I'm happy to share the ways we're finding to deliver (SOLUTION THE PROSPECT SAID THEY NEED). If right now isn't good, how does (SPECIFIC DATE/TIME) or (SPECIFIC DATE/TIME) work for your schedule?"

For salespeople in industries where sales are made entirely over the phone, having a call script mapped into sections with addendums to address common objections will not only increase your closing ratios, but also give all your salespeople a common format to use in guiding them to get the information needed to move a prospect through your pipeline. It's the difference between doing something occasionally well and consistently doing it right. It's also the difference between using hope and using systems.

You'll find the latter is the category that gets you and your company what it needs to be Bulletproof.

After you've mapped out discovery questions and objection responses in your call script, your next task is to train yourself and your salespeople in its use. We'll be adapting Bulletproof training systems in the next chapter to ensure your salespeople are familiar enough with their scripts to use them quickly and ensure they don't have to rely on them indefinitely.

CHAPTER 11

Leveraging Training Systems

AS A NEWLY minted US Marine, I was stationed at Camp Lejeune on the coast of North Carolina.

In a post 9/11 world, the Marines around me understood we would soon find ourselves in deserts, jungles, and mountains engaged in actual combat. We saw others cycling back from combat operations overseas given a few weeks off, and then saw them placed into instructor roles to ensure the rest of us would have the most up-to-date tactics and strategies to ensure *our* return home as well.

If this type of training occurred within sales teams, it would look like having top performers regularly train junior salespeople on exactly what is, and isn't, working.

Why would military leadership take their most experienced Marines, Green Berets, Navy SEALS, and Air Force pararescue forces 'off the line' and put them in instructor roles?

They understood a critical lesson that Bulletproof teams regularly put into practice:

It's better to bleed in training than on the battlefield.

Anthony Iannarino says it in a much friendlier way when he refers to the mindset necessary to overcome the inevitable challenges salespeople encounter in their careers: "If you want to ruin your career in sales, simply say, 'It can't be done.'"

Sales managers preparing their salespeople understand the power of training for scenarios ten times more difficult than what their folks will likely encounter. Being prepared for a scenario that's 10X more difficult than what they'll likely encounter ensures success in environments that are always unpredictable and rapidly changing.

While preparing Marines could have been done in a classroom setting, instructors understood it would be better to mirror the actual environments those Marines would be operating in. Instead of classrooms, we trained in simulated cities, complete with multi-level buildings, blind corners around streets, and plenty of positions where a sniper could hide and do a lot of damage. Instructors wore the same clothing as the civilian populaces we'd encounter on deployment and acted as they'd just seen the civilian and enemy populace behave while their 'trainees' patrolled the mock city streets.

Using the systems described *and* the training system we'll go over in this chapter will allow you to create some of the highest-performing salespeople in any industry. How?

Few organizations take the time to systemize their pipeline flows, outreach cadences, and the campaigns those systems live within. Fewer standardize their templates and call scripts. Fewer still integrate those tools into training designed to prepare their salespeople for *tougher conditions* than they are likely to experience with prospects.

The Prepping for Tough Prospects System

Trigger: When onboarding new salespeople and/or getting existing salespeople spun up in use of call scripts, messaging templates, and campaign systems.

Bulletproof Impact: Training that mirrors and even exceeds the worst conditions ensures that when salespeople do encounter stressful situations, they will be able to execute. Applied to sales, this means salespeople have already faced the worst attitudes, objections, and toughest prospects in role-play before revenue is on the line with actual prospects.

How do we prepare our salespeople for tougher conditions than most prospects will present?

As part of my 'spin-up' in preparing to deploy, I accompanied Marine infantry units on pre-deployment training missions. Often these missions would involve sending whole platoons of Marines to facsimiles of Middle Eastern cities erected on military bases. The Marines set to deploy would start by watching a team of experienced instructors enter one of the buildings, clear it of enemy combatants, and exit cleanly. These instructors not only worked together like a well-tuned watch, they were like engineers that build watches.

The Marines in training would then attempt to mimic their instructors' every step, hand signal, team movement, and vocal cue. Eventually, they would be able to perform the same movements in the same amount of time as they navigated through the buildings. Only then would they be inserted into a building whose layout they didn't know, and that would require them to improvise based on the scenarios they'd already dealt with. These final scenarios would force them to innovate, basing their behavior on the systems they'd been taught.

This type of 'forced innovation' was a regular part of training. How was innovation *forced* in these scenarios? Instructors would plant mock improvised explosive devices in cabinets, hide in rafters, and even act like hysterical civilians just to get close enough to the Marines to do damage – all tactics they'd seen used again and again on their recent deployments.

How does this type of real-world, progressive training differ from the training most salespeople receive? I've actually seen salespeople handed a product manual, a group of 'leads' on a card, and sent on their way to sell. Basically, they were just left to their own devices. There's a better way to train than hoping our salespeople figure it out on their own.

Systemizing Success with Prepping for Tough Prospects
Whether you are training a new salesperson or getting veteran salespeople spun up on Bulletproof selling, walk them through this training regimen:

1. Review the pipeline and objectives of each vertical

While it would take specific knowledge to explain how to use your particular CRM, it's imperative that you and your salespeople understand your prospects' pipeline flow, as well as how to access and launch the campaigns that comprise it. When prepping our clients' salespeople for success, I take the time to walk salespeople through the structure of their pipeline verticals and what the defining characteristics of prospects are in each vertical.

For instance, salespeople should be able to describe each of the following stages of a prospect's buying journey when prompted with the deal stage and be able to share what moves a prospect closer to becoming a client:

Cold Outreach: In this stage, we don't know who the decision makers are. When we find a decision maker, they move to the Decision-Maker Identified vertical.

Decision Maker Identified: Here, we know the DM (decision maker) in these accounts, but they haven't been qualified for budget, challenges that our product or service solves, or buying timeframe (if that applies). Once we find out their budget qualification, challenges, buying timeframe, and decision-making criteria, we can move them to Pre-select if we can't drive a sale or meeting today.

Pre-select: These high-value accounts have been qualified for budget, decision maker(s), buying timeframe, decision making criteria, and challenges they're experiencing that our product or service solves. Basically, we're waiting for a budget to become available and know when that will likely happen. Prospects leave this vertical either by us driving a meeting or by moving backward to the DM Identified vertical if a prospect becomes unresponsive.

The test: Once salespeople say they understand the structure of the pipeline they're managing, ensure they can tell you what qualifies an account to be in each vertical and what account activity – or lack of activity – moves them forward or backward in the pipeline.

2. Walking through each campaign's steps

As you walk salespeople through each campaign's outreach cadence, ensure they see you or their trainer execute each campaign task within your CRM and enter a record of the task having occurred. Walking salespeople through a campaign's steps while they watch means launching each campaign on a 'test prospect,' then marking call tasks as complete. It also means locating email templates within your CRM when prompted to send a particular email and accessing, customizing, and sending email and social media messages from within the CRM or transferring those templates to direct messaging platforms on social media.

The test: To ensure salespeople properly manage campaign tasks during this kind of training, I have them 'fire' a campaign on an account and walk me through each task as if they were actually performing it. While the cadence of a campaign system may have weeks in between each contact point, I have trainees complete one task, assume the time has passed in the campaign, complete the next task, and so on until the campaign has run its course.

3. Conducting outreach and using the call script

As part of training client's sales teams, we have salespeople roleplay phone calls. As the trainer, we play the role of the 'prospect' and present objections clients' salespeople often hear, including expressing annoyance at being interrupted. We do this a half dozen times or until we're comfortable with salespeople running the script without needing to read its opening questions verbatim. While it's not necessary for a salesperson to be able to recall all objection responses from memory, it is essential they can show us they know how to access them while on a call using the search function available in any online word document.

The test: In the course of call training, give salespeople an objection you know is addressed in your script. See how well they can locate the objection and respond while maintaining conversational flow, while also using it in a way that doesn't sound like they're reading it from the page.

4. Model success

Next, have salespeople listen to you or your senior salespeople make actual calls to prospects while using the call script. Your salespeople, even those with didactic memories, will need to see you use the call script in action to ensure they understand how it works to guide the flow of a conversation as you confirm or discover a decision maker, uncover needs, etc.

The test: Have your salespeople track the questions and micro-objectives you or the senior salesperson used that moved the account forward in your pipeline, verifying with you whether a decision maker was confirmed, buying timeframe uncovered, budget qualified, etc.

5. Force Innovation

At this point in training, salespeople should have a foundational understanding of how to launch campaign systems on a prospect account and execute outreach tasks. Now have some of your senior salespeople play the role of 'hammerhead' prospects and throw the toughest objections and personalities at your salesperson-in-training on a mock call.

The test: Can your trainee leverage the script you've created even in a stressful conversation? Can they still achieve some micro-objectives on the call even if a sale wasn't possible? Did they innovate any objection turnarounds on the 'tough prospect'?

6. Operate on their own

Next, have your salespeople make calls to prospects while you listen to the conversation and take notes on what the salesperson misses or blows past, as well as buyer information they stumble upon. If you notice a particular type of personality or question is tripping up your trainee, take the time to dry-run those questions and prospect personality types until you're confident they can handle them on the next call.

The test: At this stage, your salesperson should be able to ascertain decision makers, buying timelines, budgets, challenges, decision-making processes, etc. and flow through objection responses. Once a prospect call is complete, salespeople should know where the account needs to move next within the pipeline and when the next task is set to fire on the account.

The above system may take 20+ hours for a minimally viable salesperson to be trained in the use of campaign systems, scripts, and templated messages. Why, with the high turnover rate among many salespeople, would a manager take that much time to onboard a salesperson who may not work out? Great training is one of the inescapable elements of great organizations, so let's address this important question.

There's a famous quote that even Richard Branson loves to use but couldn't properly attribute, so I'll mention it here without attribution as well. Two business leaders are chatting and one asks:

"What happens if we invest all this time into our people and they leave?"

The other replies, "What if we don't, and they stay?"

Let's pause and look at how far you've come with your sales team or in standing up a Bulletproof selling system in your own organization if you've been following the steps we've outlined so far. You've defined a pipeline made up of the stages your prospects move through, stood up a CRM or more effectively utilized the one you have, created campaigns with systemized, omni-channel outreach tasks, templated messages to standardize best practices in communication, and outlined commonly heard objections. With those elements in play, you've built a sales machine that's previously only been available to the largest and most advanced sales teams on the planet.

Before using these systems with prospects, it's imperative to establish the check-in points that ensure your systems are being used and updated as your prospects, customers, and market change. These check-ins ensure everyone on the team is a better salesperson than they were the previous week.

It's time to revamp your sales team meetings.

CHAPTER 12

Upgrading Team Meetings

THE MOST POWERFUL meetings salespeople engage in are not the ones that put them in front of prospects, but the ones that put them in front of each other.

Sales Team Meeting System

Trigger: Calendar every week with sales team; can be live, virtual, or hybrid mix.

Bulletproof Impact: Gathering salespeople to not only review overall goals and pipeline movement, but also to report on any changes or challenges they've encountered since the last team meeting that may affect existing sales systems or cause system updates. These meetings are the capture mechanism for Lessons Learned and give sales leaders an opportunity to flag accounts for individual attention with their salespeople.

As I surveyed sales teams in a variety of business models, I was surprised how many sales managers *didn't* gather their salespeople very often. Their reasoning, which is sound on the surface, is that they wanted their salespeople in front of prospects and not wasting time in meetings. While that is a sound strategy if our goal is to create a bunch of cowboys and cowgirls who don't act as team members, Bulletproof sales teams thrive *because* of their team meetings.

Let's look at the reasons the highest-performing teams on the planet fight to be in briefing rooms before stepping out of the gate, and then we'll transfer those reasons into a meeting format that delivers the same value to your salespeople. If you were to sit in a Bulletproof briefing in any of the teams I studied, you might come away with these notes:

- Started at scheduled time.
- Someone was clearly in charge of directing the meeting and ensuring it stuck to the agenda.
- An overview of the strategy was presented to set context.
- Objectives of that strategy were delivered in clear, concise language with specific delivery timelines and individual accountabilities.
- Any objectives carried over from previous meetings were revisited to ensure they stayed top of mind.
- Sections and departments reported on any activity or intelligence that would be valuable in achieving the team's objectives.
- Past experiences were discussed as new ideas and plans were presented.
- Clear courses of action were formulated to adapt the team's objectives to any new information.
- Individuals in the room owned responsibility for ensuring new directives were completed on time.
- Clarifying questions that pertained to that meeting's plan were asked and answered.
- The next meeting time and place was set.
- Meeting adjourned on time.

Because these types of meetings guide participants from the strategic to the tactical, they are incredibly useful in catching potential problems early. The majority of Bulletproof sales huddles are actually spent capturing what's working and what's not, then ensuring changes are made that mitigate or eliminate problems *before* they cause lost sales.

These sales huddles are designed to provide useful information to salespeople, and that means the information has to be relevant. That's why I advise our clients conduct sales huddles on a weekly basis. These are not performance reviews. Those can wait for a quarterly or bi-annual meeting. The weekly sales huddle is instead a snapshot in time of current pipeline flow and active opportunity review. For sales managers who are hesitant to meet more frequently than monthly with their salespeople – or meet with them at all – rest assured that if the format of this meeting is followed and your salespeople are shown how to come to the meeting prepared, sales huddles don't need to take up more than a half hour a week for the entire team. As someone who personally manages salespeople, who in turn manage hundreds of accounts and millions of dollars' worth of pipeline value, I can attest that it's possible to accomplish the meeting in a half hour each and every week.

And perhaps the biggest benefit of a Bulletproof sales huddle?

They get us better prepared to get back out in front of prospects and sell!

Systemizing Success with Sales Team Meetings

Below, I've shared an outline of the sales huddle we've adapted from briefings witnessed across Bulletproof teams around the world. You'll see explanatory notes below items to give context. A simplified agenda without the explanations is included in Bulletproof Resources section at the end of the book so you can model this type of sales huddle for yourself.

Weekly Sales Huddle Agenda

Opening:
➤ Set start and stop time of the current meeting
   (*This prepares participants to be physically and mentally present for a set length of time.*)

Objectives Review:
   (*It's important that the individual salespeople and the team as a whole are kept up to date on how close they are to achieving collectively assigned objectives. For many sales*

teams, this will be a financial goal mixed with contact or call goals. If a sales manager has weighted sales goals across their team based on tenure, territory, or other differentiators then it is acceptable to combine the goals of the team to provide an overview of where the group or company is in meeting overall goals.)

➢ Review primary sales objective:
(These are the traditional 'sales metrics,' usually expressed in dollars of product or services sold. It is here that any 'closed deals' that occurred since the last meeting are reported.)

➢ Review secondary objectives:
(These are the secondary or tertiary micro-objectives that lead to presentations, proposals, and closed business, such as decision makers identified within accounts, buying timelines, budgets discovered, etc.)

Pipeline Growth:
(This can be the individual dollar or deal growth of each salesperson's pipeline since the last meeting or the overall dollar or deal growth of the team's collective pipelines.)

Upcoming Opportunity Review:
(This is where the individual or sales team reports on the deals and dollar value they expect to come 'open' for purchase decisions from buyers in the next week or month. This provides the sales manager with an opportunity to flag any necessary accounts for individual follow-up coaching with salespeople. Individual review of upcoming potential sales is not required during the meeting unless a challenge was encountered or is anticipated by the salesperson. As a sales manager myself, I'd much rather discover a potential problem before a sales presentation is made to a prospect.)

Active Opportunity Reviews:
(This is where any deals that have proposals out or are in the final stages of purchasing are reviewed. Rather than get too granular here, I only ask clients' salespeople to list the next outreach step and date they have planned with the decision

maker on deals that meet size or value benchmarks, understanding that we must always own the next step of the sale and not leave anything to a prospect saying, "We'll get back to you when we're ready to purchase." This ensures deals closest to generating revenue don't fall through the cracks, and if next contact steps are reported publicly to the team, this holds salespeople accountable for executing follow-up tasks.)

Individual Account Reviews:

(This is the portion of the meeting where salespeople bring up any challenges or questions they have about particular accounts in any stage in their pipelines. If meeting as a team, it's encouraged to have senior salespeople give input if they have action-oriented solutions that have worked for them. Critical to reviewing any account challenge is that it is captured for entry in the next portion of the meeting, Lessons Learned. I go so far as to prohibit any account problem being presented that doesn't generate a Lesson Learned and/or a system change. Simply solving a problem for one salesperson today without incorporating that solution into systems all but guarantees that problem will resurface with that same – or another – salesperson in the future and will need to be re-solved, or worse, go unsolved and cost revenue and commissions.)

➢ Post-Mortem on lost deals
(If a deal goes as far as generating a proposal and is lost, this is the portion of the meeting where salespeople bring those accounts for review to the group. Instead of it being a reason to shame someone, it's a massive learning opportunity for every salesperson. As with individual account reviews, every lost deal by any salesperson should generate a new Lesson Learned or reiterate the importance of using a system already in place. For sales managers leading larger teams, it is perfectly acceptable to establish deal value criteria for this section to ensure dozens of small-value lost deals don't take up the majority of the sales huddle.)

Continuous Improvement:

➢ Lessons Learned
(We've devoted an entire chapter to this system, so refer to that information for a full explanation of the Lessons Learned system and its database.)

➢ Record courses of action (COAs) for new scripts/systems to handle challenges or experiences
(This is also captured in the company's Lessons Learned database, which we cover in a future chapter.)

➢ Review last week's Lessons Learned that changed systems
(After capturing new Lessons Learned in the team database, review the previous week's Lessons Learned and any actions generated to ensure updates are underway for the team's systems.)

Accounts Receivable Review:

(Depending on your business model, this is where a sales manager reviews any spiffs or commissions due to the salespeople if that information is shared publicly. If your company prefers to keep this information private and between the sales manager and salesperson, omit this section.)

Wins for the Week:

(Prior to closing the meeting, this final portion is one of the most critical parts of the agenda and should never be overlooked. It is here that the sales manager has the opportunity to end the meeting on a high note by highlighting the successes of the team or individual salespeople. If you choose to highlight individuals, ensure you rotate the spotlight each week so that everyone has a chance to be recognized – even if it's just for moving an account into a deal stage or pipeline vertical they had previously struggled to achieve.)

Close + Next Meeting Time Confirmed:

(It is here that the sales manager confirms the place and time of the next sales huddle so the team can get it on their calendars and ensure other meetings don't interfere.)

While it may seem like a lot packed into one meeting, the length of the sales huddle I've outlined above is determined by time both the meeting's leader and salespeople spend in preparation.

Until you've run one of these team meetings according to the outlined agenda and with proper preparation, it's difficult to describe the change that occurs within a team. First, salespeople will be amazed that so much could be covered in such a short amount of time. Second, they'll be more amazed that issues and challenges were openly shared and received by their leadership. When these weekly huddles become part of your organization's routine, salespeople will want to be in the room, because just as with Bulletproof teams in combat, what's shared in these meetings can massively affect every individual's success. When your salespeople see their recurring issues addressed and systems stood up to ensure those problems no longer hinder them, they'll be converts to the value of this impactful meeting.

At this point in our journey, you've been exposed to more systems than most sales teams on the planet even know are available. Whether you're underlining passages as you go or capturing your rollout plan in a separate notebook, what we're going over in the next chapters will have an immediate impact on your sales efforts because it's all about systems to use when engaged face-to-face or ear-to-ear with prospects.

The danger in any sales improvement book or program is not that you or your salespeople don't use the information you learn to close more business. Rather, it's that the information is only used once, generates results and is then forgotten. Unfortunately, a lack of systems across most sales teams virtually guarantees any new 'tricks' or 'tips' see limited use. The systems we'll walk through in the coming chapters, while extremely impactful on their own, will not become standard operating procedure if there's not a larger system comprised of a pipeline and its campaigns to ensure all the prospect-facing systems are consistently used.

Now that you understand the importance of placing any prospect-facing technique within a larger system that contains a trigger event, is repeatable, improvable, and measurable, let's leverage systems to get better results with prospects. What would it look like to be Bulletproof when entering our prospect's offices?

- Every satisfied client would be on call to personally sing your praises to new prospects
- *Your company* would be the one teaching prospects how to price, evaluate, and buy your product or service from any competitor in a way that makes your company the only obvious option
- Discovering the upper range of your prospect's budget early in the sales conversation and never having to sell the 'base model' of your product or service again

In the following chapters, we'll be covering techniques that produce those outcomes, and when used within a Bulletproof selling system, occur during *every* sale, regardless of the tenure of the salesperson or the amount of prospects they're pursuing.

CHAPTER 13

Enlisting Clients
To Join Your Sales Team

BULLETPROOF SYSTEMS DO a more effective job than anything else in eliminating competition because few competitors are using systems of any kind. Building on that advantage, systemizing past clients to help us make future sales does an excellent job in leveraging them as partners in developing new business.

Who do decision makers choose to buy from, especially when their reputation is on the line? They buy from companies that have successfully sold to others like them and have clients with their same job titles, responsibilities, and P & L concerns. That is how a provider can become entrenched in an industry without advertising, marketing, or even providing a superior product or service: Their buyers spread the word. While that's a great sales strategy if you have decades of history in an industry, it can also be engineered by a startup or ambitious sales team in this Bulletproof system.

When dealing with decision makers, it's imperative to remember what influences us also influences them. Have you ever been in the market for something that had a lot of different varieties, quality levels, vendors, and reputations to select from? With that many variables to sort through, most of us abandon the hours of research required and do what other humans tend to do: We look at what our peers say.

Enlisting Clients as Partners System

Trigger: Occurs as soon as a client has received your product or service and is pleased with its results.

Bulletproof Impact: Every past client enlisted as an advocate to tell other decision makers why they should take time to meet with and buy from you. Captured in text and video, client testimonials provide reasons to reach out to prospects with value-added information and represent an opportunity to grow their own networks.

How do we leverage reviews of our product or service in a way that puts every past client on call as a selling partner?

Testimonials.

But not the kind you're probably familiar with.

Let's look at the ways most companies use testimonials, if they have them at all. Most of the time, they are in written form, composed by random people within our clients' organizations, and rarely leave our company's website, meaning that unless a prospect stumbles upon them, there's little chance they'll be seen by anyone. Ever. On top of that, few testimonials feature the picture or even company name of the people who wrote them, which often raises doubts as to their authenticity.

But let's say that *your* company is doing an exceptional job with your testimonials and bothers to include a headshot and the company name of the person who left you the review. There are still gaps in leveraging one of the most powerful tools in your Bulletproof sales kit. First, the question anyone has when perusing a testimonial about your product or service is, "Does the person in the testimonial have my responsibilities, concerns and duties?" Few testimonials, even those that have headshots and company names, bother to address this. The second way most companies drop the ball with their testimonials is making them completely passive. Unless someone stumbles upon them while visiting your website, they're not likely to be seen outside your IT or marketing team.

With the right kind of testimonial, in the right format, and used in the right way, we have the potential of recruiting every decision maker we've ever done business with as an on-call representative for our own sales and marketing team.

To accomplish it, we'll need to change three things about the way most companies gather and leverage testimonials: format, source, and location.

Testimonial Format:

Video content is the primary source decision makers – or anyone these days, for that matter – consume when it comes to content. There's a reason YouTube is the second most popular search engine on the planet. To turn every decision maker we serve into a personal advocate for our business, each salesperson on your team should be trained and tasked with creating testimonials using video footage and post-delivery interviews with their buyers as part of their post-sale system – a simple process we'll cover below.

Testimonial Source:

Some companies believe in treating their products like Amazon.com listings, thinking the more '5 star' reviews they have, the better. Unfortunately, most businesses' testimonials are a waste of time. Why? Not everyone in a prospect's company is responsible for making the decision to purchase our product or service. Decision makers want to hear from their peers so they can mitigate risk. While the opinion of a blue-collar employee from the warehouse or supply chain might be better than no testimonial at all, it takes a lot of them to sway an executive's decision to take a risk. Alternatively, it often only takes one other executive in their industry singing your company's praises to sway a buying decision.

Testimonial Location:

Before we dive into how to systemize the use of these high-level testimonials, we need to cover perhaps the most overlooked aspect of testimonials, especially video testimonials: their location, specifically **where** a prospect views them.

While there are many paid video-hosting platforms that allow for gathering metrics, controlling follow-up videos, and presenting calls-to-action, most salespeople and organizations standing up their own testimonial video strategy will be starting with the free platform for hosting their videos: YouTube.

YouTube is great for a lot of things, especially videos of cats doing silly things. But it's not the best resource for salespeople to send prospects to when leveraging testimonial videos within outreach campaigns. Testimonial videos have to be hosted *somewhere*, and they can definitely be hosted on YouTube. However, they don't have to be *viewed* on YouTube. The danger in sending a prospect to your company's YouTube channel or dropping a YouTube link in an email is that not only will prospects see your video, they'll also see thumbnails of every other video YouTube wants them to see while your video is running. That's way too many distractions for even the most focused prospect. Instead, we have the ability to control what a prospect sees around your testimonial videos, including other products and services you offer that might interest them, the ability to schedule time to meet with your salespeople, and of course, the option to see other testimonial videos from satisfied clients with their job titles. The best part? Where a prospect *views* your testimonials is a resource your company likely already has in place – your own website.

Your company's website is the best piece of standalone marketing you have for whatever you sell, and if you could get more qualified prospects to visit it, the more awards your marketing team would win. There's a billion-dollar industry called Search Engine Optimization (SEO) that exists to accomplish that very thing. While SEO is great, all it can do is help get an interested visitor onto your company's 'real estate,' and even the best SEO won't help with websites that don't convert prospects to conversations that generate sales. As part of your Bulletproof system, your sales teams can be the ones driving qualified traffic to your company's website as part of their sales campaigns.

Systemizing Success with the Enlisting Clients as Partners System

Your IT and marketing department can easily create parentless pages, which are pages that cannot be found within your website's menu drop-down choices, but instead require a unique URL to access. Here, you can create a page specifically for each testimonial video, with links below it to schedule time with one of your salespeople, fill out an inquiry form, or whatever next steps your sales require. Testimonial videos can then be linked from where they're hosted on YouTube and appear on your website's parentless pages. We recommend not hosting more than one testimonial video per parentless page, as you'll want your salespeople to be able to title them something like: 'A message from Jim Smith, VP of Operations at the Widget Manufacturing Corporation.' You can definitely load your collective testimonials onto a single page that is accessible from your website's main menu as a mega-credibility video roll.

Regardless of how many testimonials you post onto any website page, make sure it's *your company's website* you're sending prospects to for testimonials. When a prospect finishes viewing a message from someone like them, you want them exploring all the ways your company helps companies like theirs, not exploring what silly cat tricks have been released that week on YouTube.

Capturing Decision-Maker Testimonials

To create these kinds of high-level recommendations, your salespeople should schedule periodic check-ins with client accounts to ensure everything is working properly, gather referrals, and of course to get video testimonials. While the ramp-up and onboarding time of some products and services are longer than others, the important thing is that your sales team decides on a reasonable timeline to check in with new clients to fix any problems and secure testimonial footage, making that a scheduled part of your client onboarding system. The interview itself can be as simple as asking decision makers for a 30-45 second interview with their name, job title, why they chose your company, and what they'd tell another decision maker who's thinking of buying your product or service.

When we started coaching our clients in how to secure these testimonials, we advocated that they start with a video interview with their decision maker in a head-and-shoulders frame. Testimonial effectiveness skyrocketed, however, when clients began grabbing 'B-roll,' or footage of their product or service being used, that could be shown on the screen *while the decision maker being interviewed* shared their thoughts. If you never have contact with the end-user of your product because of your supply or distribution channel, your B-roll can be footage of your product being delivered, installed, or serviced by your team. The end product of this system is a mini commercial that's not you talking about how awesome you are, but rather the person responsible for purchasing sharing their thoughts *along with* footage of them and their employees using your product or service.

The video can be captured with a smart phone, and the editing can be done by an employee with basic video editing skills or cheaply outsourced. If your company sells to decision makers in various industries or geographies, your testimonial videos can be categorized, segmented, and targeted to similar decision makers. To accomplish that, catalog your testimonial videos with tags for industry, type of decision maker, type of product or service, etc. and make them available to *all* your salespeople.

How should we coach clients in what to say on these testimonials? As most folk aren't used to being on camera, we've discovered that it's often easiest to provide willing clients with a quick script that can be quickly read to a decision maker before recording begins:

"Hi, this is (name), and I'm the (job title at company). We recently hired (the salesperson's company) to help us (achieve

the value proposition the product or service delivers). Here are the ways they delivered and exceeded our expectations .... If you're a (job title of decision maker) and thinking of (achieving more in the area your product or service deliver results), it's definitely worth your time to meet with the folks at (the salesperson's company) to learn more."

Using Decision-Maker Testimonials

Once you and your team have gathered a few of these high-level testimonials, we advise our clients to load each of them onto its own parentless webpage on your business' site, in addition to creating a page where they all appear. Unless a company policy prohibits salespeople from leveraging each others' accounts as references, all video testimonial links should be loaded onto a master sheet along with the decision maker name, company name, and industry.

These video testimonials can then be programmed as part of the value-added messaging within email templates throughout your campaign systems – both as stand-alone messages and as potential introductions to other decision makers. They can also be included in follow-up emails after a conversation with a decision maker has occurred. Don't make the same mistake with your video testimonials you might have been making with your generic testimonials by leaving them to languish on a website page.

Video testimonials, like all testimonials, are most effective if prospects with similar job titles *actually see them*. Don't leave that to chance.

While enlisting past prospects onto your sales team is a standalone system worth the price of this book many times over, it pales in comparison with our next system, where we'll be showing you how to train current prospects to eliminate every competitor in your market.

CHAPTER 14

Training Prospects To Eliminate Competition

ONE OF THE most powerful things a company can do is set the standard for excellence in their industry. When we were still carrying MP3 players around, consumers measured all of them against the features and benefits of the iPod. It is possible to recreate that success even in a commodity market, and it happens through educating potential buyers about the things they *should* be asking as they make purchasing decisions. In the Bulletproof teams I studied, the educational material we used to guide our decisions were called Field Guides.

Field Guide System – Hard Copy Version
Trigger: When a salesperson discovers a qualified decision maker within an account, a hard-copy and digital/video field guide should be sent.

Bulletproof Impact: Train buyers how to vet, select, and source your product or service, and to do so using specific criteria that your company provides to them. Effectively establish your product or service as the choice no competitor will be able to match. Educate prospects on the options your company has available before your first sales meeting, increasing conversion.

The sole purpose of these field guides is to educate prospects on how to vet, negotiate, prioritize potential suppliers, save themselves money, and get the most value possible when purchasing a product or service. Of course, Bulletproof salespeople leveraging this powerful system have the opportunity to build their differentiators throughout their field guides. This positions their company as the only obvious choice to consider. Once you develop your own field guide it can be sent at the next prospect interaction across both new and legacy accounts.

These field guides – which can span written and video mediums – are so effective because very few companies take the time to develop them and fewer ensure they end up in the hands of decision makers.

Systemizing Success with Hard Copy Field Guides

First, let's review the hard copy version of this tool. For paper or PDF field guides, I recommend these not take up more than one page per product or service for ease of use. Additionally, they should be available in a PDF version for ease of transmitting electronically. We want these field guides to actually be printed out and used by prospects instead of languishing in an email folder. If you use direct mail or handwritten snail mail as part of your outbound campaigns, these field guides can be printed and included in your next prospect mailing *once a salesperson has set context for them with the prospect.*

It's critical that context be set for what a field guide is and how to use it before a prospect sees it for the first time. If these field guides show up in your prospect's world with no context from your salespeople, they'll lose their effectiveness and likely go unused. We find this conversation to be an easy one when prepping a prospect for a field guide:

"Now that we've got our next appointment set, I just remembered we developed something I can send over immediately that will save you time and money as you look at different suppliers for (product or service). We understand that while we're in the business of delivering (product or service), most of our clients aren't. Too many companies in our industry aren't educating folks on the levels of quality and service available, so we developed a field guide for our clients to help them purchase a (product or service). It's an easy one-page guide that will walk you through the questions you should be asking potential suppliers and even answers to listen for. Let me confirm your mailing/email address and I'll send it today."

Of course, sending anything to a prospect to review, especially a field guide, is a perfect reason to set another follow-up call to see if the field guide was useful or if the prospect has any questions prior to your next scheduled appointment.

Who should write and create your field guide? It's always better if your field guide can be co-authored by you or your company *and* someone outside your company who is or has been responsible for purchasing your product or service. For instance, our 'field guide for buying a keynote speech' was authored by both myself and a certified meeting planner, one of the titles many of our buyers have.

What you want prospects to think after speaking with any other supplier or vendor of your product or service is, "Compared to the folks who sent me this field guide, others don't measure up." As you formulate the introduction and questions prospects should ask about your product or service, ensure that you phrase your questions and answers in a way that positions your company as the only one who *can* provide that level of service or particular differentiator.

Begin by outlining in one paragraph the importance of the decision in selecting the product or service, how it impacts brand perception, employee/customer retention, etc. Next, emphasize how this decision could impact the person's reputation within the company and in their market. If a poor supplier is chosen, the repercussions go far beyond the lifespan of the product or service. Finally, share that if a supplier doesn't meet at least the minimum requirements your field guide shares, they're likely not the right vendor.

Now onto the questions and answers that make up the bulk of the one-page field guide. The ones listed below are generic and give direction for how to customize to your industry. Of course, feel free to add any questions that position you as the only obvious choice as a supplier of your product or service as long as they fit onto one page. In the examples below, you'll see the questions in standard type and answers or insights in italics.

Keep in mind these questions are written from the perspective of the prospect, intended to be used as an interview guide for their conversations with other salespeople they talk to about your product or service:

- When meeting with a potential supplier, are they familiar with our industry, employee, and client challenges?
  (Your potential supplier should ask about what outcomes you're looking for across each area the (product or service) impacts.)

- Does the potential supplier inquire about our past experiences with the (product or service) early in the conversation?
  (If they don't, they may not be interested in surpassing your expectations with their product or service)

- Does this potential supplier ask if the purchase of this product or service will be considered by anyone besides myself?
  (The best suppliers are willing to provide specific information to all interested parties as they understand this decision impacts more than just one person in the company).

- Does this potential supplier offer to provide more than just the (product or service) as part of their offering?

(If they're not offering additional value for the price you pay, you may be getting shortchanged.)

Specific questions to ask:

[*Note*: these are industry and product or service specific, so customize these to what you're educating prospects to buy as you are creating your field guide]

- Does this potential supplier offer to customize the (product or service) to our company, employees, and audience?
  (They should offer to interview at least 6 people within your organization as part of their post-sale delivery preparation to ensure the (product or service) meets your exact needs.)

- Does this potential supplier offer to assist us in rolling out the (product or service) to our employees/clients?
  (The best suppliers will offer to create – or help you create – a rollout campaign to ensure maximum use, efficiency, and implementation of the (product or service).

- Does this potential supplier offer to assist us in implementing the (product or service), including producing training videos for us and our customers?
  (Your supplier should offer to assist you with getting the (product or service) established in your company to ensure you get maximum ROI on your investment.)

- Does this potential supplier mention the technical support that comes with (product or service) as part of their base package?
  (Superior suppliers include personal support for (product or service) even with the basic package.)

- In what ways is this potential supplier willing to customize the (product or service) to our company's needs?

(If they aren't willing to customize the branding, software, and training to your specific organization, you may be purchasing a generic solution rather than one built for your needs.)

- How will this potential supplier ensure that every one of the individuals – staff OR customers – in my organization who utilizes (product or service) has the support they need to be successful?
  (The best suppliers have tangible ways to ensure that everyone who uses (product or service) in your company has the support they need to be successful.)

- Does this potential supplier offer follow-on courses or services to ensure our organization/customers continue to receive the benefits of (product or service) long after purchasing?
  (If your potential supplier isn't willing to include follow-on support after purchase, you may be dealing with a supplier more interested in the sale than in your success.)

After the overview and question/answer portion of the field guide, you can include a brief outline of your company and of course, contact information for your salesperson. If you make this concise enough to fit onto one page, you'll have created a powerful tool for your prospects to use if they're considering other suppliers. If you want to take this system a step further and really stand out from your competition, you can be the one educating your prospects with video field guides.

Field Guide System – Video Version

Trigger: When a hard-copy field guide is in place, video field guides should next be developed.

Bulletproof Impact: As with hard copy field guides, these video field guides train buyers how to vet, select, and source your product or service, and to do so using specific criteria that your company provides to them. Expanding on the effect of hard copy field guides, these video field guides educate prospects around the specific questions they should be asking of all potential suppliers.

Marcus Sheridan covered the topic of educational content marketing in his excellent revised edition of *They Ask, You Answer: A Revolutionary Approach to Inbound Sales, Content Marketing, and Today's Digital Consumer.* A video-based field guide is similar to what Marcus calls the '80 percent video,' a video that encompasses answers to 80% of the questions your salespeople get about your product or service.

These videos can be studio-produced with footage from your manufacturing facility, supply chain, customer installation sites, etc. or simply shot with one of your salespeople talking into the camera of their smartphone. As it applies to educational-based content, done is better than perfect, and your video can always be re-shot and improved down the road. Regardless of production quality, these videos should walk prospects through the questions your salespeople hear most often while also positioning your company as an educator, guide, and top-flight provider of your product or service. While it's best to survey your salespeople for the questions they most commonly hear from prospects before filming your video field guide, here are some common categories that you can make specific to your product or service:

- Product or service: Is the product or service even right for me and my company, given our goals?
- Alternatives: What are alternatives to the product or service, and what are the pros and cons of each?
- Price: Why does the product or service have different price points?
- Differentiator: How should a prospect select a company to do business with? What should they look at and ask for in the areas of experience, customization, customer support, warranties, and follow-up?

Systemizing Video Field Guides

The length of a video-based field guide is based on the complexity of your product or service and the attention span of your average prospect, but we've found that 3 minutes tends to be a good target point. However, these guides can be as long as 15 minutes if your product or service is complex and highly customizable.

These field guides can live individually on your company's website as 'parentless' pages your salespeople can direct prospects to when a question arises about price, installation, warranty, etc. They can also be combined into a series of videos posted on a single page as a resource page or FAQ page. If a salesperson hears a question from a prospect that is answered in a field guide, sending a link to the field guide is a great response, while also setting a follow-up call to discuss, of course.

Field guides ensure you are always in the running as a potential supplier, not because your company is always the cheapest option or even the most well-known. Rather, they work so well because so few salespeople systemize helping prospects make great buying decisions. Unfortunately, most companies simply aren't willing to build additional service offerings to support what they sell or don't realize that many value-added services could be the difference between making the sale or losing it.

Of course, you may have read the questions and response prompts we went over and thought, "We don't have anything like that in the way of customization, support, or service for what we sell." That may be true as of today, but it also gives you a clear checklist of things your sales, customer service, and support teams should get busy building. Creating any of those value-added items can be done on a shoestring budget and with little to no capital investment (and we cover ideas for those items in-depth in our upcoming chapter on the Bulletproof Offer System). I know because we've built those value-added offerings in my company and in client companies. To deliver on all the items you're telling prospects to vet other suppliers against, your entire organization will have to hold itself to a high standard and continually be on the lookout for ways to ensure you go above and beyond what anyone else in your industry is doing.

That's what great companies *should* be doing, after all. The field guide is one of the more complicated Bulletproof systems to create, but even its role is to encourage decision makers to meet with you and your salespeople. It's that meeting, whether conducted over the phone, virtual chat, or in person, that makes or breaks the sale. Bulletproof systems don't leave that meeting to chance and neither should you.

CHAPTER 15

Prepping For Bulletproof Sales Meetings

WHILE PREPARING TO step into missions, military troops showed up an hour before a mission was set to kick off for a pre-mission brief.

They willingly showed up to this meeting because it often ensured more people would return alive. Rather than being high-level strategy sessions, these quick briefs went over important timelines and tactics for coordinating efforts between other units, along with reviewing changes going into effect from the latest Lessons Learned captured around the globe.

It's easy to understand that having the most up-to-date information is important. However, these pre-mission briefs also served to reorient everyone on their upcoming mission objectives. In quickly changing environments, how a mission is accomplished often changes with the weather, geopolitical shifts, and even local traffic patterns. Having the most up-to-date information was often the difference between success and failure.

Unfortunately, few sales teams take the time to brief salespeople for *their* crucial missions: sales meetings. Sales leaders simply hope things go well when their folks meet with important decision makers or when closing large deals. If we wait until *after* a sales meeting occurs to review potential problems and failure points, the train has already left the station. That's using hope as a sales strategy, and we're long past that in our Bulletproof journey.

Sales teams who fail to plan are planning to fail, which is why the sales meeting brief is so critical.

The Sales Meeting Brief System

Trigger: Occurs just before scheduled sales meetings with qualified decision makers.

Bulletproof Impact: Ensures salespeople have all information and materials needed to ensure success of upcoming sales meetings. Includes a top-line review of the prospect, that prospect's company, and any pertinent information that will help establish rapport. This custom-built review goes over important information that will aid salespeople in being perceived as professional solution providers.

In our clients' organizations, we teach and recommend conducting a sales meeting brief before important buyer meetings. It saves lives in combat and saves sales in business. Of course, briefing <u>every</u> outbound call with a salesperson before they picked up the phone would drastically limit the number of calls they could make. That's why parameters should be set for when this type of sales meeting brief occurs. At the very least, they should happen before calendared appointments with confirmed decision makers.

More important than *when* these briefs occur is that they *do* occur. Start by defining your team's highest-pressure, highest-stakes meetings by size of opportunity, complexity of deal, number of decision makers involved, etc. and immediately begin briefing before those meetings.

Systemizing Success with the Sales Meeting Brief System

Because this brief occurs just prior to a scheduled sales meeting, it should be built into the systems your salespeople use once a meeting is booked or placed on their calendars. For instance, if a sales meeting is scheduled on a salesperson's calendar at 9am, a sales meeting brief appointment should appear just before it at 8:45. Whether built into your scheduling system or manually entered by your salespeople, if this isn't scheduled on their calendars prior to the meeting time or before the salesperson departs for a physical meeting, it likely won't happen.

To systemize the structure of this brief, let's first review the players involved. In this quick meeting, only the salesperson – or salespeople – meeting with the prospect(s) and the sales manager need attend. If you have inside sales reps whose responsibility is to gather information and schedule your salespeople's meetings, involve them as well as they'll have been the last point of contact with the prospect.

Second, the place. If you operate a central office where your salespeople are required to physically report, this briefing can be done in a quiet office before your salesperson or salespeople depart for the prospect's office or join prospects on the phone. If your team is geographically dispersed, the sales meeting brief can be quickly completed on the phone or before the salesperson and prospect enter a virtual meeting room or phone call.

Third, the time. As with all meetings, the shorter they are, the better. Two and a half minutes is standard for a sales meeting brief; they're that quick. Again, these briefs are not for discussing company margins, sales quotas, or lengthy account histories. Like football players reviewing the next play they're about to execute, this brief covers the next few minutes of the game and ensures everyone on your team is on the same page.

Fourth, the format. Preparing for the brief ahead of time ensures it is efficient. This might require an account scrub, looking through CRM notes, and even reviewing social media channels for pertinent information about the prospect that will help establish rapport. Obviously, that data can't be collected during the brief if we're trying to conduct it within a few minutes. Fortunately, this prep can be accomplished during off-calling hours or the day before the meeting. In fact, we've found it most effective if the briefing data is loaded into the sales brief calendar entry that appears before the sales meeting. This ensures it's readily available for review during the brief.

Here's an example of how down and dirty the briefing can be. Seriously, it's one paragraph. If your sales leaders don't have the time to prep one paragraph that could make a massive difference in the success of your salespeople, and if your salespeople don't have 2.5 minutes to get their heads in the game, then *hoping* everyone executes at a high level may be a better option for your sales team.

In this briefing scenario, the salesperson set the high-value appointment, but hearing the information repeated from the sales manager confirms what the salesperson already learned from the prospect and also ensures account information was added into the CRM or calendar notes correctly. This is what a sales meeting brief sounds like:

"Ok John, you're going to be meeting with Susan Smith via phone in a few minutes. According to your notes, Susan is the VP of operations of Acme Widget Corp, whose top line was $150 million last year across 350 employees. You're going to be discussing our HR software platform and determining which version best fits her company's needs. We've been in contact with this account for a year and a half, and this is the first scheduled meeting you're having with her. Because her budget is qualified for our premium service offering, our asking price will be $45,000 with a target of $42,000. Any discounts below $40,000 require manager approval. I checked with our delivery team and we have the resources available to get that installed as early as the first of the month. According to LinkedIn, Susan has been in her role for three years, lives locally in the bay area, and her profile shows her as being active on a few community boards. You should have your Bulletproof Offer prepped for that premium package and ready to send via email before your call begins. As a reminder, we've experienced a delay in email sending due to server issues, so you'll want to send any mid-session emails a few minutes before you need her to receive them. You'll be dialing in on 555-555-5555, extension number 37. Any questions?"

While those few sentences don't seem complicated, there's a lot of valuable information there. Note that the brief reviews who the salesperson is meeting with, that prospect's job title, the revenue of their company, number of employees, the type of package the salesperson will be recommending as their initial offering, history of the account, number of prior meetings, budget ranges, delivery/installation timelines, and even professional and personal information about the buyer that might be pertinent to the conversation. Even the call-in number is reviewed so the salesperson can confirm the numbers they're dialing.

How did we learn to advise our clients research and prepare all of that information ahead of time? A lot of lost revenue from *not* reviewing that information before our own sales meetings. To define your own team's briefing items, your salespeople and sales teams can whiteboard the fundamental things that are 'good to know' and 'need to know' before sales meetings to ensure they are included in your sales meeting briefs.

Additional items unique to your industry and company will quickly become apparent during your sales meetings *debriefs*, which we'll cover in an upcoming chapter. As a general starting point, we've found the following items to be essential for review to get salespeople's heads in the game before important sales meetings:

Name of players involved

Everyone's favorite word is their own name, and Bulletproof salespeople leverage every resource they can to establish rapport. Because a calendared appointment will always involve at least one person from the prospect's organization, it's vital to confirm their name and the names of anyone else from their organization who may be attending.

Product or service line to be discussed

Discovery questions to determine product line usually occur prior to a sales meeting, so it's imperative that a prepared salesperson have one or more specific solutions in mind that they intend on discussing with the decision maker(s) in the meeting. This also allows narrowing of service lines, discount levels, promotional offerings, customization and delivery capabilities, installation specifics, etc. While additional information may reveal an entirely separate product or service line is a better fit, it's still imperative that the salesperson goes in prepared with all the information needed to sell the most likely product or service line this prospect could benefit from.

Date and location of service and delivery (if applicable)

If your product or service's sale depends on you or your salesperson or your delivery team being physically present on a certain date if the sale is made (at a wedding, event, conference, etc.), it's a good idea to go over those details prior to the meeting as well to confirm calendar availability. Decision makers will not respond kindly to their time being taken for a meeting only to discover your company is unavailable on the specific date your product or service is needed.

Anticipated Budget

It is useful to re-orient the salesperson conducting the meeting on total deal value. This is also the place where the sales manager can confirm the discount window the salesperson is authorized to work with and any timebound promotions or discounts your company is offering. If your company leverages deal values to determine which prospects receive preference in limited product or service offerings (for instance, holding multiple dates for service delivery with preference going to the largest deal), overall budget factors into the preference your salesperson can offer their prospect in delivery priority. Again, your salesperson is absolutely encouraged to discover additional budget during their sales meeting but knowing what the minimum range is will qualify this meeting as worth taking seriously and is needed for prepping your Bulletproof Offer, a topic we'll discuss in the next chapter.

Phone number or location of meeting and who's making contact

It's surprising how many sales are lost because a salesperson thought a prospect was calling, the prospect thought the salesperson was calling, or someone confused which virtual meeting room they were supposed to be in. It's imperative to review who is supposed to be dialing or meeting with whom. While this may seem like a mundane issue that professionals would handle by default, we also know that a mis-entered note in a CRM about a meeting can cause a mistake that creates an irreversible impression in a prospect's mind. If your salespeople can't be trusted to fulfill a simple agreement like showing up at the right place and time, what does that say about what it's like to do business with your company? For that reason, simply confirming the meeting's details will at least ensure salespeople don't make a mistake that could at best delay your sale, and at worst may kill it entirely.

Company details

These will largely be dependent on the industry you're selling in and the types of customers your company sells to, but knowing the decision maker your salesperson is meeting with works for a company with international presence that could benefit from your product or service in every one of its locations is a valuable piece of intelligence to know before the meeting as it could impact the volume discounts your salesperson might offer. Conversely, knowing your salesperson will be meeting with a startup company with limited budget but that is willing to entertain a multi-year contract for your product or service because of expansion plans may also affect pricing. Most of these details can be gathered during the initial discovery questions or through online research.

Details about the players involved

If your salesperson was able to connect with the decision maker(s) on social media prior to your meeting – and why wouldn't they? – then it is valuable to review any personal or professional details that might help establish rapport. Like an intelligence dossier delivered to a Bulletproof team prior to a mission, understanding your prospect's educational background, career history, and any social media interests will accelerate rapport and therefore, the sale.

Necessary materials

If your company relies on pricing sheets, draft proposals, or product samples, now is the time to confirm those things are ready to present, available to send via email, or packed in the salesperson's kit. While we advocate for the 'less is more' approach to schlepping things around, if your prospects expect your salespeople to have a pricing sheet or product sample, ensure your salesperson has it on hand.

Possible contingencies

While no one can plan for every possible outcome of a sales meeting, it is a good idea to review the most likely objections and outcomes and review what the salesperson's next steps will be in the event those contingencies occur. The middle of a high-pressure sales negotiation where revenue is on the line is not the time for a salesperson to play jazz with their pricing structure, overcoming objections, or adjusting value-added offerings. In the same way a fighter pilot is not expected to crawl onto the wings of their jet if an engine catches fire but instead practices what to do during an engine flameout, our salespeople should review contingency plans *before* they're needed.

Any questions

It's at this point, the final part of the pre-event brief, that the salesperson can ask any *clarifying* questions. These might be around discount levels, customization options, or whatever else your salesperson needs to know to better prepare for success in the meeting. It's not a time to ask about why they're presenting to this prospect or go over issues with their CRM or anything else outside of the upcoming meeting. Any questions asked this close to 'game time' need to be about the play they're about to execute and nothing else. If the sales manager conducting the meeting has any Lessons Learned that are so new they haven't been built into systems but will likely aid success in the upcoming meeting, mentioning those changes last often means they are the first thing the salesperson remembers when meeting with their prospect.

With a solid sales meeting brief that triggers when a buyer meeting is scheduled, your salesperson will be better prepared than most of your competitors and will be able to confidently present your product or service, all while knowing the names of the people they'll be meeting with, having an idea of the product or service lines that may be a good fit, how soon they can be delivered or installed if purchased that day, whether specific delivery or install dates are available, size of the anticipated budget range that will assist them in putting together any preliminary proposals, how and where they'll be meeting to ensure the proper person calls or visits the right location, details about the organization to help the salesperson understand the depth and length of current and future sales, and details about the decision maker(s) involved that can help establish rapport and provide talking points.

When all that information can be prepped ahead of time and delivered in less than a few minutes, what salesperson wouldn't be better prepared for success? A good pre-event brief often reminds both the sales manager and salesperson of a missing piece of paper or pricing strategy they would have otherwise overlooked. More than anything, it sets the standard on a Bulletproof team that sales leaders own as much responsibility for success as their salespeople.

While preparing for your next sale will ensure you and your salespeople are using all the tactics and insights you've gleaned from this and other sales training programs, even they pale in comparison with the tactic of *delivering* more value than anyone else while maximizing revenue for your sales team in every sale.

That's why our next Bulletproof selling system is so powerful – it delivers both more value than many prospects are even aware is available and simultaneously captures more revenue. It's the proverbial win-win, and when I mention 'more revenue,' I'm not talking about a small percentage uptick. Companies that have implemented the next Bulletproof system have regularly seen an increase in actualized revenue per sale of more than *300%*. That's how powerful it is. To utilize it will require a bit more confidence than some members of your sales team may have at the moment and will also fly in the face of what many of us have been taught about our pricing structures.

Let's dive into this next system by taking a visit to our nearest luxury car dealer. What we learn there will impact our sales systems in ways we might have never thought possible.

CHAPTER 16

The Bulletproof Offer

INSTEAD OF PLAYING by a decision maker's terms, which would involve cutting our product or service to its bare-minimum price and conceding all your value-added services just to get the deal, what if we treated our sales conversations more like a Bulletproof team would – minus kicking in doors, of course?

It would likely look a bit different from the way your sales team is presenting their product or service's options and pricing today. Because few readers will have had experience clearing a house, let's review an experience many of us have had: purchasing a vehicle. Top auto salespeople have a clear understanding about maximizing the value of the transaction to their prospects while bypassing what a stated or unstated budget might be.

While it may be true your prospects would like to pay as little as possible for what you sell, a few other things are also true about the folks who buy from you: they probably have more budget for your product or service than what they'd prefer to pay you, and they're willing to pay more than their stated budget if it speeds up results and delivers more of what they want. Car salespeople understand this about every person who walks through their dealerships, which is why the finance department is the biggest moneymaker in any dealership's business model.

Why would a perfectly reasonable and otherwise fiscally responsible person willingly spend tens of thousands of dollars more than intended for a depreciating asset? A lot of it has to do with the pricing strategy we'll reveal in our next system.

When I went shopping for my first luxury car, I wandered into my nearest dealer's showroom and was greeted by a friendly salesperson. This salesperson and I exchanged names and, after learning I had wandered into the right establishment and was in fact looking for the type of vehicle they sold, we walked over to the newest vehicle available. Of course, it was conveniently parked inside the showroom. We sat in the vehicle while the salesperson walked me through all the things that made their brand unique in the luxury auto space. I was encouraged to test, fiddle with, and experience everything this top-of-the-line car had to offer. Knowing I could customize this new model to my specifications, I was excited about negotiating and asked what the sticker price on this beauty was.

I was informed, "For the 47 new features in this car you've said you love, plus the factory warranty, it's only $85,000."

That was a bit outside my price range, and I let the salesperson know. What happened next opened my eyes to the possibility of increasing revenue our clients could capture by borrowing and adapting this unique pricing strategy. Because what happened in the dealership next was not a long sigh, shaking of hands, and a parting of ways. Without missing a beat, the salesperson asked me what features I'd seen that I'd be willing to live without.

"I don't need the Corinthian leather," I responded. "And the claw that pops out of the seat and massages my scalp in traffic seems like a safety hazard ..."

Did the salesperson *once* ask me what my actual budget was? Nope. Instead of asking what I intended to spend that day, which would have meant showing me the rust-bucket the dealership's mechanics threw into a ditch out back, the salesperson walked me from the air-conditioned showroom to the cars outside. We sat in a car that had all the features I'd said I didn't need. You'll never guess, but *that* car was too expensive, too! We played this game until we finally found a vehicle for me that had all the features I needed and could afford, even though it was *not* a vehicle that met the budget I thought I would spend.

"But wait," some savvy readers will be chiming in, "my buyers don't work that way. They make all vendors submit their pricing, and then choose the cheapest option."

I know that statement isn't true, but there are still salespeople who believe it and continue to wonder how they lose deals to companies charging more. Let's dispel the myth of cheapest-price-always-wins, then we'll return to this system and explain how it can work in your sales team's model, too.

Take a look around you, right now. At the room you're in, the clothes you're wearing, even the town you live in. Unless you're sitting on the dirt, naked, in Wichita Falls, Texas (named the cheapest US city to live in during 2020), you aren't making purchasing decisions based solely on price. While you may not buy the most expensive version of everything you want, you also aren't choosing the cheapest, either.

The people who buy your product or service aren't buying the cheapest option of everything, either. Despite how they might hem and haw about price, they *are* willing to spend more money than the cheapest version of your product or service *if* it paints a faster path to their goals.

Unfortunately, this is something many salespeople overlook. How do I know? If you're like most of the sales teams I've worked with, you have 'tiered' offerings and call them something witty like 'gold,' 'silver,' and 'platinum.' While you may have evolved enough to customize those tiered offerings for different prospects and placed variable pricing on them, if you're starting your sales pricing with tiered pricing or 'packages,' then your sales team is leaving a tremendous amount of revenue and commissions on the table.

At no point in my car buying journey did a salesperson sit down with me and offer me 'pricing options' to help me select the right vehicle for me. Why? They knew if *they* made price more important than value, they'd be cutting their commissions off at the knees. Instead, they worked with me to craft the ideal value package I wanted and then removed items from that to meet the upper tier of my unstated budget. Of course, the ceiling I thought I had on my budget wasn't the actual ceiling. There were unexplored levels of my budget they happily showed me how to access.

The challenge with tiered pricing of any product or service is that we're inviting our prospect to choose a cheaper option than the one that will most benefit them. Whatever we're selling, it's because it will aid someone – or some organization – in being more successful. If someone wants to travel from one coast to another, for instance, we could sell them a bus ticket, train ticket, or airplane ticket. The fastest and most effective means of travel is an airplane, and it's also one of the most expensive options. Why? It's one of the most efficient ways to cover distances! Otherwise cost-conscious people willingly spend hundreds of dollars more each day for faster, more efficient travel.

People and organizations are <u>always</u> willing to pay more to achieve their desired result faster and more efficiently.

Salespeople often ask at this point in our workshops, "If we're not offering tiered pricing, what should we be offering?"

Glad you asked. It's called the Bulletproof Offer System.

The Bulletproof Offer System

Trigger: To be used in the middle of a sales meeting with a confirmed decision maker after strategic goals and ideal outcomes have been discussed.

Bulletproof Impact: The ability to add more value to clients than anyone else in your industry while capturing up to 3 times as much revenue per sale. Ensuring your product or service has the highest chance of ROI for your clients and making your company a long-term partner in their success.

The tactics we'll share in this chapter are predicated on you dealing with a qualified decision maker – attempt this system with a gatekeeper or information-gatherer at your peril. If your industry's model usually requires you to deliver initial pricing to a procurement officer or finance department before a decision maker meets with you or you salespeople, then definitely submit tiered pricing to get the meeting. Of course, the most successful salespeople in even those types of industry are still the ones that are able to get meetings with decision makers prior to ending up in the procurement office.

To execute this Bulletproof system, we'll be compiling all the value-adds we would put into our 'platinum' package and making that our first offering. Don't be concerned if your prospect can't afford your highest-tier package. We'll also be using the same step-down sales tactics many of us have experienced at auto dealerships to get our prospects into a custom-made version of our product or service at a price that maximizes our revenue and their results.

Like savvy auto salespeople, we should never start sales conversations by asking about the ceiling on our prospect's budgets. Few will reveal actual budget limits until they understand how our product or service helps them achieve their goals, which is why asking about budget early rarely yields honest answers. Instead, we should uncover needs through discovery questions and match solutions to our products and services before ever mentioning price.

We'd never walk into a doctor's office and listen to all the surgeries they could perform, with pricing models, if they hadn't even performed an examination, would we? And yet, so many salespeople lead with price in their conversations.

Instead, we advise our clients to leave price out of their sales conversation until they know enough about their prospect's needs to make qualified recommendations. Occasionally, we are all pressed into a hard stop by prospects saying something along the lines of, "Before I answer any more questions, I need to know what this costs." Our response is always humorous and points out that neither of us, the salesperson or the prospect, knows enough to confirm an exact price. We'll say, "We've provided (product or service) at price points ranging from free to $1.5 million dollars. My sales manager likely wouldn't approve free and I'm guessing you haven't allocated $1.5 million. Once we learn a little more about your organization and the outcomes you're looking for, we can definitely generate pricing options."

At that point, we 'parking lot' the budget issue and immediately move on to the next discovery question. While we have past client sales to justify the use of $1.5 million as a deal value, you can replace that with whatever your largest sale has ever been or what others in your industry charge for their largest offerings.

Although that script works 95% of the time, we have seen clients' sales teams occasionally encounter a buyer who can't move forward unless they have a dollar figure in their heads. In that case, we advise to use the minimum viable package you offer, phrased in this way: "Our basic/standard package for this is $X, but to be honest, we don't sell many of those because our clients find that once they understand how we can accelerate the results of our product or service with some unique differentiators, they want those included. To understand which of those differentiators would be a good fit for you, let me find out..." and then roll into your next discovery question.

To get started building your Bulletproof Offer, gather the items offered in your tiered pricing packages together. This may be as simple as combining items across all packages for your product or service lines into a running list, or it might require some strategizing with your customer service and delivery teams. At the most basic level, you're answering the question, "If we could sell a version of our product or service to someone with an unlimited budget, what could we include in the package and what would we price it at?"

Although the exact items and pricing in your Bulletproof Offer may differ based on the number of locations or number of employees in your prospect's organizations, it shouldn't be too difficult to create a few 'Bulletproof Offer' packages, depending on what an unlimited budget would look like to the groups of prospects you're pursuing.

Just as auto salespeople have a system for how they present their premium-level vehicle and then step-down their prospect into the highest priced vehicle that meets all the prospect's needs, there is a system we must use in presenting our Bulletproof Offer if we don't want to overwhelm decision makers. While it may seem counter-intuitive – and likely is the opposite of what your sales team is currently doing – follow me if you'd like to see closed deals and revenue spike.

Systemizing Success with the Bulletproof Offer System

Note the focus of this section is presenting your offer, not when to send your pricing. Few decision makers can equate a product or service with its price until they understand how that product or service helps them achieve their goals. Too many salespeople are quick to send over pricing sheets, which only commoditizes what they sell and invites prospects to pit your competition against you.

In using this Bulletproof Offer strategy, savvy auto salespeople don't start by sitting someone down in an office and walking them through the 867 customization options available with line-item pricing for each. Similarly, don't come out of the gate in a sales conversation with all the things you or your salespeople can do for a decision maker, the three-dozen value-adds you can build in, and your trendsetting warranty. Features are meaningless to a decision maker in the beginning of a sales conversation.

Instead, ensure your salespeople take the time to learn what your prospect's goals are. What areas of their lives and business are they looking for improvement or change in? Go back to the earlier exercise where we defined results-oriented benefits if you need a refresher about what to listen for. Only when a salesperson understands what destination a decision maker wants to arrive at do they have the authority to show the decision maker a map of how they can get there more quickly and efficiently though their product or service.

The next thing needed to succeed with this system comes during the sales call or sales meeting itself. We and our clients found this system to be most effective if the Bulletproof Offer options are emailed in the middle of a virtual negotiation or slid across the table during an in-person sales meeting with a qualified decision maker. Why? If the items in this offer are provided too early, it's easy to get lost in the tactics of how each item works and its individual pricing. Not to mention the decision maker has no idea which items will most quickly help them achieve their specific outcomes. It's the role of a professional salesperson to be able to assess a decision-maker's desired outcomes and recommend the quickest and most efficient route to get there.

The Bulletproof Offer email or item sheet is simple and free of distracting language. We use the following template in the email we advise our clients to send during their qualified sales conversations:

{{FIRST NAME OF PROSPECT}}-

As we're discussing, these are the things we are doing to ensure (product or service) makes a positive impact for your organization in creating a better experience for {{EMPLOYEES or CUSTOMERS}} that begins before we even deliver the (product or service), makes a massive impact while it's being implemented, and delivers a return on your investment long after purchase:

<u>(Value-added things we do before delivery or installation of a product or service):</u>
Item 1

Item 2
Item 3
Item 4
Item 5
Item 6

(Value-added things we do during installation or initial delivery to ensure adoption and implementation):
Item 1
Item 2
Item 3
Item 4
Item 5
Item 6

(Value-added things we do after delivery or installation to ensure continued use and benefit):
Item 1
Item 2
Item 3
Item 4
Item 5
Item 6

Thank you,
(Signature line)

Again, those items are sent without individual pricing and are simply described. Your salespeople will not be reading each item as a laundry list. Instead, once the email is sent or the paper is handed over, salespeople highlight one or two items in each of the three sections and explain how *those particular items* ensure the outcomes the decision maker specifically said were important. This might sound like, "Because you said getting folks registered early was important, you'll really appreciate that we include pre-event marketing material, videos, and custom articles for your organization's newsletter as part of this product or service," which can serve to drive home the value of these examples.

At no point in the Bulletproof Offer conversation is your decision maker made aware that there are any other packages to consider *besides* this one. Your Bulletproof Offer should become your standard offering when meeting with qualified decision makers. Here's where the magic happens by not using tiered offerings: Not only have you demonstrated that you or your salespeople understand this buyer's outcomes enough to make specific recommendations, you've also included things no other competitor has shared with them are even available as most companies ascertain budget first, and then in a desperate effort to close the sale, only present their package that meets that budget. Additionally, the Bulletproof Offer allows us to discover the upper range of a prospect's budget. You can pull items for your Bulletproof Offer right from your field guide's question and answer list as well – things that are low-cost to your company to deliver but add massive value and impact to your buyers.

If you're still wondering how to come up with all the items for a Bulletproof Offer, ask yourself, "If someone was willing to pay me three times as much as I'm currently charging for what I sell, what could I throw into that package to help with their success in using my product or service before, during, and after delivery?"

Some low-cost and high value options:

Before delivery

Interview members of their team to ascertain potential challenges in using your product or service, create installation guides and videos, create articles for their organization's use to introduce the new product or service to internal audiences, include a briefing call with key stakeholders to prep for rollout.

During installation/rollout

Flexible scheduling to minimize disruption to their operations; customizing the product or service to their locations, company branding, or color preference; 24-hour communication with installation and rollout teams to address any challenges; online course to speed implementation and adoption.

<u>After delivery/rollout</u>

Follow-up coaching sessions or webinars to answer any questions; follow-up online course to ensure continued use of the product or service and ROI; free or low-cost updates, service plan, or warranty; individual coaching sessions with key stakeholders.

Of course, many of the items that will be most impactful to include in your Bulletproof Offer are currently in the heads of your salespeople and customer service team. They're likely things already being done but that haven't been systemized. Perhaps they're things your team has heard about peers in your industry doing but your organization hasn't implemented yet. Decision makers don't know what the standard for excellence is if it's the first time they've invested in your product or service or if they've only dealt with salespeople offering the bare minimum, so it's our job as Bulletproof salespeople to educate them.

The time a salesperson dwells on a few items in their Bulletproof Offer shouldn't amount to more than 30 seconds. Again, salespeople should only highlight those items they know will meet the specific needs they've uncovered through discovery questions. Only if the decision maker asks about other items on the list should they be explained, and again, every effort should be made to tie those items back to the strategic solutions the decision maker mentioned they were seeking.

Because this system allows us to add more value than competitors, eventually a decision maker will ask, "How much does all this cost?" At that point, your salesperson is welcome to present whatever your 'platinum package' price is, the price your organization can deliver all those items for that builds in an extremely healthy margin for you. Let's say your Bulletproof Offer price is $20,000, and your baseline package with just one or two of the options on your list can be sold for $5,000 with a healthy margin. When the Bulletproof Offer price is mentioned, it should be along these lines: "Because you mentioned the need to solve X, increase your revenue by $Y, and make sure it happens in Z timeframe, we can build all of this into a custom package for you for $20,000."

One of two things will happen when that price, which is four times the base package in our example, is presented. If your salesperson has done a great job of tying key items back to solutions the decision maker is looking to achieve, they may ask, "Where do I sign?" However, the second outcome is the prospect saying, "That price is way outside our budget."

The sales teams we coach in this system *love* to hear "That's outside our budget" when leveraging their Bulletproof Offer. We teach them to respond, "I totally understand; that's a big investment to make. Tell me, what items *can you live without* and I can see what items we can remove to get to the number you're thinking of. What was that, by the way?"

That question does a few things that allows this system to work so beautifully.

First, it reveals the upper end of your prospect's budget. They might have walked in thinking they could purchase your product or service at the standard $5,000, but now they know you have the capability to provide so much more to ensure efficient rollout, a great experience using the product or service, and continued value long after installation or delivery. It's unreasonable to ask for all the items on the Bulletproof Offer list for $5,000. Whereas many sales negotiations might end with the decision maker asking the salesperson to "Go sharpen your pencil and get back to me," this strategy requires the decision maker to instead sharpen *their* pencils so they can maximize value to their organization for the maximum amount of budget they have access to, if budget for your full Bulletproof Offer isn't available.

Second, when a salesperson makes it clear that items will need to be removed to provide your product or service at a lesser price, it opens the potential for the salesperson to become a partner to the decision maker, ensuring maximum value is included in the custom package that's built for this project.

Third, this system showcases a standard of excellence in your deliverables few competitors will be able to match. Those items aren't presented as the most expensive 'tiered package' you have, but rather the standard you offer to everyone interested in your product or service. It's up to the prospect to decide which options are needed for the budget they have.

What happens after the upper end of the decision maker's budget is determined and necessary items are carved away to produce a customized package that they can afford? In other words, how do we get ink on the page and close the deal with this system? Another advantage to using the Bulletproof Offer is that it leverages scarcity, urgency, demand, and social proof.

Scarcity

Many of the value-added items your salesperson and decision maker agree upon may be limited in quantity or availability. If your decision maker wants to lock those value-added options into the proposal, a shortened decision-making timeline can be established.

Urgency

Because many of the items in your Bulletproof Offer require planning on the part of your company to deliver, if the prospect wants them, then time is of the essence. To ensure customized items like courses or manuals can be included, the jointly-agreed-upon proposal with the options the decision maker *can* afford needs to be executed and sent to accounts payable as soon as possible.

Demand

If your organization has its hands full building and delivering other Bulletproof Offers, then your salesperson can absolutely leverage that fact to drive an accelerated decision. Although it's a variation of the scarcity tactic above, it is especially effective if you're also building and delivering a Bulletproof Offer package for one of your decision maker's competitors or peers. To ensure this new decision maker gets a place in line for the items they've deemed essential to success, the sooner a decision is made, the better.

Social Proof

A subset of 'delivering for a peer in the industry' tactic above, a salesperson mentioning the name of a similarly sized client or competitor in the industry who chose all or a few of the same options currently being considered is also effective in driving more prompt buying decisions.

What's the result of using a Bulletproof Offer system that makes it so valuable to both salespeople and clients? Because it is truly customized to a client's needs, it takes something that might otherwise be price-fixed or a commodity and transforms it into an offering that can't be purchased off the shelf. If your salespeople are selling an intangible service, it gives the service a concrete blueprint that allow a prospect to map the research, delivery, and follow-up they're investing in that might otherwise be invisible or nonexistent. Above all, it allows salespeople to provide more value than any competitor is willing to and customizes even the most basic product or service to a prospect's unique needs. Interestingly, it also weeds out buyers only interested in paying the cheapest price for the minimum level of service and quality.

How do your salespeople consistently come up with new ideas to add to your company's Bulletproof Offer, and what happens to ensure if they close a deal with it that everyone else on the team benefits?

While selling is where the action tends to happen, it's after the sale that real progress begins. The way to leave hope behind permanently in your sales strategy lies within the lessons salespeople learn when conducting outreach, presenting their offers, and after meeting with prospects. The next chapter is focused on the system you can use to find, refine, and systemize those lessons to make your sales truly Bulletproof.

CHAPTER 17

The Sales Meeting Debrief

IF YOU'VE SEEN the movie *300*, the dramatic story of the Spartan stand against the Persian army at the gates of Thermopylae, you may remember the scene where King Leonidas is departing Sparta with his group of 300 warriors, headed to certain death. His queen said something that was often told to departing warriors in Greece. In its original Greek, it was, "E tan, e epi tan."

Translated into English, it means, "Return with your shield or on it."

For ancient and modern warriors, not returning home doesn't constitute failure *if* their sacrifice was a worthy one. While salespeople are not heading into actual battle, they are battling each day for commissions, battling against the ignorance or apathy of some prospects, and battling against everything else their prospects have on their schedule besides an interruption or sales meeting.

And yet no matter how tight our pre-sales meeting brief is, no matter how flawlessly we execute our Bulletproof Offer, we still won't win them all. Alternatively, our next sales meeting might close the biggest sale of our careers. Regardless of the outcome of a single sales meeting, what we *can* bring back, regardless of a meeting's outcome, is a lesson. Whether a sale was made or not, being better next time is a salesperson's version of returning 'with their shield or on it.'

A requirement of Bulletproof salespeople, then, is to return from every sales meeting with ways they can improve, *especially* if they made the sale. If we pay attention to challenges encountered in our outreach and on every sales call, we'll never be short of ideas to make our sales teams better for the next sales meeting.

If we want to have any hope of taking on better-known competitors, operating with less resources than our peers, or (gulp!) selling higher-priced products and services than they do, we must take the time to examine sales conversations for ways to improve what we do. There is a way to Bulletproof our future sales meetings:

Enter the *Meeting Debrief.*

The Sales Meeting Debrief System

Trigger: Conducted immediately after a sales meeting.

Bulletproof Impact: Capturing exactly what went right and wrong with each qualified sales meeting and capturing those lessons in a way that benefits the entire team. Ensures salespeople are using best practices, and regardless of whether a sale was made, ensuring success with future sales.

This system allows salespeople and sales managers to ensure the systems, training, and tools provided for their sales meetings were brought to bear, that all necessary information about the prospect was discovered and confirmed, that the salesperson owns the next step of contact, and that anything learned from a success or setback is captured for everyone's benefit. If an item was missed during the meeting, the sales meeting debrief will capture it for that salesperson's future improvement, as well as for potentially salvaging that account before the sale is lost.

It turns out, every Bulletproof team I've studied across industries – whether in the military, wildland firefighting, law enforcement, sports, performance, business, or sales – used a debrief system to capture not just their losses but also their wins. While we covered the format and flow of an operational debrief in the book *Pivot Point: Turn on a Dime Without Sacrificing Results*, the sales meeting debrief is unique in the world of sales so let's systemize it for your team.

Systemizing Success with Sales Meeting Debriefs

For debriefing high value sales meetings, the sooner the debrief occurs, the better. That might mean your salesperson calling in as soon as they get into the car after the sales meeting or as soon as their sales manager is available. The more time that passes between a sales meeting and its debrief, the more Lessons Learned will be lost, which is why it's imperative the debrief happens quickly.

If, as a sales manager, you're wondering if it's worth adding these debrief sessions to an already-packed schedule of administrative duties, consider this: the debriefing system allows us a window to see our sales teams' behavior in front of prospects and even gives salespeople the leverage to salvage potentially lost sales after their sales meeting ends. As a sales manager myself, I can think of no better use of my time than learning more about how my salespeople are interacting with prospects during critical sales meetings and helping them improve. Here's what the debrief system accomplishes from the perspective of a sales leader:

- Ensure salespeople are following company standards of professionalism
- Ensure decision makers are confirmed
- Confirms the decision-making process
- Confirms a buying window or timeline
- Confirms the number of employees or customers that could benefit from the product or service in that company
- Discovers the strategic and tactical objectives of the buyer

- Reviews the prospect's ability to accept our Bulletproof Offer pricing model or learn what items need to be removed to meet the budget
- Ensures value-adds or upsells are offered to ensure faster ROI
- A follow-up date is confirmed in your CRM so your salesperson maintains the next step
- If additional decision makers or buyers are discovered, additional account profiles are created for future outreach

If you could *ensure* your salespeople were accomplishing each item above in every sales meeting, it's almost a certainty closing ratios would increase. It's also a certainty that your salespeople would begin consistently doing the things on that list they may not consistently be doing today. What gets measured gets managed.

The Sales Meeting Debrief Format

As soon as possible after the sales meeting, hop on the phone with your salesperson and run through your debrief checklist (we've provided a sample checklist in the Bulletproof Resources section at the end of this book). This debrief meeting is all about speed and efficiency – any systems that need updating can be captured and saved for the weekly sales huddle and Lessons Learned program. Keep this meeting focused on the sales meeting that just occurred. Your checklist will include items specific to your organization and industry, but here's a basic example to model. We've entered background information in italics to help explain why each item is important to review.

Using a checklist format keeps the debrief short. For instance, when a sales manager asks, "Did we confirm whether we're dealing with a sole decision maker or a committee?" the salesperson's response should be, "Yes, Bob said he was the sole decision maker." or, "Yes, Bob said that he is the chair of the selection committee, a group of 5," or "No, I didn't confirm whether he was the decision maker."

The more succinct we can train salespeople to be during these debriefs, the more value they'll get out of them and the faster they'll get back to driving more sales meetings. Let's dive into the outline of the sales meeting debrief:

Debrief Format

Review Primary Objective:

Confirm decision maker and decision-making process, and secure agreement to send our Bulletproof Offer proposal to the buyer with a decision deadline.

(It's imperative that you set a #1 priority objective with your salesperson prior to the sales meeting and then review it when the meeting concludes. This lets them know what to focus their efforts on.)

Review Secondary Objective:

Confirm decision maker and decision-making process with follow-up date to provide any missing information, and get permission to send Bulletproof Offer proposal for consideration with a decision deadline.

(If the sales meeting does not generate a request for a proposal, it's also imperative that the salesperson knows what success can also look like – and that's securing a second meeting where any missing info can be presented and a proposal can be generated.)

Did we:

_____Confirm whether we're dealing with a sole decision maker or committee?
(This will be important when sending any proposals, scheduling follow-up meetings, etc.)

_____Confirm the decision-making process?
(It will be important to discover how a buying decision will be made as it will affect follow-up steps after the meeting.)

_____Confirm buying timeline?

(When will they plan on making a decision? If it's tied to a certain date, we need to know that in planning specific follow-up events.)

_____Confirm number of employees or prospect customers our product or service could affect?
(A question that is often overlooked, this data will be critical if we enter negotiations for our Bulletproof Offer. We need salespeople to be able to refer back to specific metrics in helping prospects understand the impact of our product or service across their organization and even down to their own customers.)

_____Discover and confirm objectives for our product or service?
(Critical in justifying any investment, we want to ensure our salespeople take the time to ask what success looks like to the prospect so we can customize proposals and any follow-up material to <u>those objectives</u>.)

_____Discover or confirm upper limit of budget?
(Critical for being able to ensure a deal's value is accurately reflected within the salesperson's pipeline, the Bulletproof Offer system will reveal how much the prospect is actually willing to pay for our product or service even if they can't stroke a check today. That number will allow a salesperson to modify their Bulletproof Offer to give sales managers an accurate idea of sale value.)

_____Review ability to accept Bulletproof Offer pricing or the need to remove items to meet the budget?
(We need to know if the Bulletproof Offer pricing fee was accepted, and if not, what specific items did the prospect want removed to see if we could meet their budget?)

_____Offer additional product lines?
(If you have product lines that are outside the reason the prospect agreed to meet but that could also impact the prospect's objective, were they mentioned during the sales meeting? Which ones?)

_____Confirm follow-up date and time for next point of outreach?
(In line with our earlier system of <u>always</u> owning the next step in any prospect interaction, this ensures the

salesperson has a follow-up date and method listed in their CRM to ensure they don't allow the account to go stale.)

_____If going to a committee for decision, did we offer to customize a message for them and confirm what date it needed to be delivered by?
(We find that if we've met with a decision maker who needs the consensus of a committee before making a decision, it's always a good idea to produce something specific for that committee to review, whether it's a video, individualized set of proposals, etc.)

_____Is the salesperson connected to the decision maker on LinkedIn?
(If the salesperson isn't connected to the decision maker by the end of the sales meeting, they should be!)

_____If the decision maker asked for a proposal, who is moving this account into an Active Opportunity?
(Whatever you call your 'accounts receivable' process, ensure that the deal is moved into that status – the vertical of your pipeline that is closest to generating closed business.)

_____If a proposal was requested, which departments will be CC'd?
(Depending on your internal processes, some deals will need to have others tagged in for follow-up steps. Ensure that if that is the case, your salesperson understands who will need to be made aware.)

_____Were referrals requested? Received?
(For the truly dedicated salespeople out there, a first-time meeting is often the first time they have an opportunity to ask for the names of anyone else in the prospect's organization or network who might also benefit from your product or service. Contrary to what your brain may tell you, you can ask for referrals in your first sales conversation. If we don't ask, we don't get.)

_____Did we capture anything that could be considered a Lesson Learned concerning the salesperson, prospect, or sales manager? If so, what?

*(We have devoted a whole chapter dedicated to this information and what to do with it to drive change – it's **that** important. If a sales leader has the ability to be present for the sales meeting or sales call, here is where to review anything that was off-system or off-script, as well as established sales systems that could be improved.)*

Notice the flow of the debrief checklist can also serve as your salesperson's meeting agenda! Feel free to add any items unique to your product or service, industry, or sales systems in your debrief if it's critical to assessing, selling, delivering, or maximizing value of your product or service.

What If We Missed a Checklist Item?

Even after designing and using our own sales meeting debrief checklists, I occasionally miss a checklist item myself. Usually, it's because we're managing a complex sale and simultaneously discovering needs, formulating recommendations, and navigating objections. When the sales meeting is complete, hindsight does become 20/20 once we realize that we could have established a stronger position if only I had asked a specific question of a decision maker.

What do we do if we realize that we or one of our salespeople skipped over an essential question on our checklist?

First, capture it as a Lesson Learned. It's a guarantee if one salesperson is skipping an important question in a sales meeting, others on the team are also doing it at least occasionally and perhaps systemically. We'll go over the format we use to implement these Lessons Learned in the next chapter, but for now, simply make a note of it on the sales meeting debrief checklist.

Second, assess if there's time to get that missing question answered **now**. That may mean picking up the phone or walking back into the prospect's office and saying something like, "Hi Bob, yep – I'm back already! As I was going over my notes, I realized that to give you the best answers to the questions you asked about, I've got one more question …"

If that prospect is unavailable, then the salesperson needs to get a follow-up step scheduled for later that day or the next business day to get ahold of the prospect and answer any missed question(s). Assuming they conducted themselves professionally during the sales meeting and were more focused on the prospect than on themselves or their product or service, it's rare that a prospect will see this additional question as an inconvenience. If you took the time to meet with a doctor and the doctor stopped you on the way out to ask an additional question, would you find it an inconvenience or be happy to answer it in the hopes it helped with their treatment recommendations?

Capturing Lessons Learned from the Debrief

While we've devoted a whole chapter to the mechanics of capturing and implementing Lessons Learned, one of the final parts of the sales meeting debrief is asking, "Did we encounter anything that could be captured as a Lesson Learned?"

Sales meetings, whether conducted on the phone, virtually or in person, are where the rubber meets the road in any sales cycle. The sales meeting is also where revenue and the most valuable Lessons Learned come from, which is why we place extra emphasis on learning what we could we have done better. Or, having known how that conversation would turn out, what would we have planned to do differently to achieve a different outcome?

The best campaign systems, the most succinct discovery questions, and the tightest follow-up sequences in the world won't matter if they don't generate sales meetings that turn prospects into clients. For that reason, capturing anything that could have been done more, better, or differently during sales meetings is crucial.

There are three areas that serve as prompts for Lessons Learned during the sales meeting debrief. An important note is that assessing the following areas will serve your team whether the sale was lost or won.

First, Debrief the Salesperson

Ask the salesperson if there was anything they think they could have done more, better, or differently during their sales meeting.

If your salesperson needs a prompt, consider:

"If we knew the answers to the questions we asked during that sales meeting in advance or if we could review a recording of that meeting before it happened, what could we have researched, prepared, or brought with us to be more successful?"

If you, as a sales manager, were able to be present for the meeting or listen to a call recording of it, this is the time to offer your feedback to the salesperson while also capturing specific points as Lessons Learned to review during your weekly sales huddle.

Second, Debrief the Prospect

This is the time in the debrief to take the focus off of your salesperson and put it onto the prospect. Because the prospect is human, it means they share many things in common with other decision makers in your industry that you, that salesperson, and other salespeople on their team will encounter again. This is the time to ask, "What about the prospect's behavior, questions, inquiries, or background that we learned during the meeting would have been helpful to know before walking in?"

Prospect questions that took your salesperson by surprise can be captured and researched, and then responses can be built into future training, scripts, questions, and systems.

Third, Debrief the Team

Finally, turn the focus away from the prospect and salesperson and turn it towards the sales manager, the sales team, or your parent company. A great question to ask your salesperson is, "Knowing the questions you'd be asked by the prospect, what could we have provided to you that would have better prepared you for success?"

If you are injecting a sales meeting debrief system into an existing sales team with decades of combined experience, this question will quickly bring about any systemic problems your salespeople have with your company's processes, marketing material, customer support, etc. This should serve as a warning bell that to better support your salespeople in generating revenue, there are things that can be done more, better, or differently.

How to Capture Lessons Learned

We'll dive into the full Lessons Learned system in the next chapter, but you'll need a quick way to jot down notes on your checklist as you and your salesperson run the debrief. A single sales meeting could produce a dozen Lessons Learned in the early days of a Bulletproof system rollout, so simply capture the name of the account, name of salesperson, date of the capture, and what was learned as you conduct the debrief. A single Lesson Learned from a debrief can be as succinct as:

1/23/2021, ACME account sales meeting | salesperson Bill Smith. Bill realized after the meeting he didn't ask for referrals.

Once you develop a post-meeting debrief checklist and require sales managers to use them with salespeople after every important sales meeting, you'll soon have a plethora of actionable ways to improve your sales systems, beginning with how you qualify prospects, how they are contacted and at what intervals, and of course with sales meetings. Instead of allowing those lessons to live in the memories of the salespeople who experienced them and become inconsistently applied across future prospects and sales meetings – the definition of using hope as a sales strategy – they can instead be used to improve your Bulletproof selling systems. As your prospects' needs, selection criteria, and budgets shift, you and your sales team will know about it, adjust accordingly, and be able to pivot before your competitors.

The fuel of active feedback from your sales meeting debriefs, salespeople, and even feedback from existing customers is what drive teams to the top of their industry in sales, customer service, and satisfaction scores. It's what makes Bulletproof teams Bulletproof.

We've saved how that feedback creates change and keeps your systems dynamic for last; it is how all other sales systems are refined and improved. Let's dive into the most powerful continuous improvement system for salespeople on the planet –

Lessons   *Learned.*

SECTION III

*Becoming
Bulletproof*

CHAPTER 18

The Engine
Of Bulletproof Change

"I have heard those who follow the Way
travel the wilds without fear of animals.
Facing a barrage of arrows,
they remain unharmed.

Dangerous creatures find no place to claw, bite or tear them.
Weapons find no opening in their armor.

Why?

Because those who follow the Way are beyond attack."
-Lao Tzu

THAT QUOTE BY a mythical Chinese philosopher could have been written about any of the Bulletproof teams I studied across businesses or combat. What I witnessed as part of their systems was a way to *engineer* the type of cultivation Lao Tzu mentions – a way to rise above the challenges that held everyone else back.

One of the sales trainers we've referenced multiple times, Anthony Iannarino, phrased the idea of continually improving as a salesperson in this way: "To win, you have to be better than you were yesterday and better than your competition is today."

Imagine if we could engineer this type of improvement on our teams?

What would change if you and your salespeople were trained in what was working as of <u>this moment</u> in prospecting, selling, closing deals, and generating referrals in your industry?

What would happen if every lost sale was something your entire team could learn from? And if you could put systems in place to ensure no one lost a deal for that reason again?

What amount of time would be saved and number of sales would be generated if you knew that your team was measurably better every week at prospecting, eliciting interest, winning clients from your competitors, and increasing conversion?

How it would feel to have salespeople who were actively capturing successes and challenges throughout their week and willingly sharing those with their teammates to increase everyone's top line?

What might be the impact of having access to every lesson your salespeople had learned? What about being able to do that across dozens of people with decades of combined sales experience?

And perhaps the most valuable aspect for making the most of the training you've already invested in with your salespeople?

If instead of *hoping* to remember the great tips picked up in that last sales book or training program, you and your team *knew* those improvements were being utilized with every prospect, in every negotiation, and with every client from now on?

In an earlier chapter, we outlined the acronym TRIM that defines a sales system: Trigger, Repeatable, Improvable and Measurable. Yet, each of our sales systems thus far have only have their 'Trigger' explained. The reason we didn't cover the repeatable, improvable and measurable aspects of each of those sales systems is because knowing something needs to be improved and knowing how to improve it are vastly different. The Lessons Learned program we outline in this chapter accomplishes that very thing – allowing us to improve each of our sales systems and providing us with the tools to measure their effectiveness.

The teams I studied around the world who actively leveraged their Lessons Learned program had more than a 98% success rate in reaching their objectives – with life-and-death stakes. Imagine the improvement your team would have if they could query decades of experiences from every area of their sales cycle? Access to that kind of information means a salesperson would have to go out of their way to *lose* a sale. That kind of team doesn't have to hope things go well.

Let's get this powerful engine working in your sales systems.

<u>Lessons Learned System</u>

Trigger: Conducted at each weekly sales meeting, new lessons are entered by sales leaders or salespeople as needed.

Bulletproof Impact: A Lessons Learned program is the engine that fuels innovation and continuous improvement across all pipeline movement, campaigns, outreach cadence, call scripts, sales meetings, negotiations, delivery, service, and referral generation. It's an online database where challenges and discoveries can be recorded and replicated across any size team so that every salesperson can benefit from what other salespeople learn. Lessons Learned are a way to measurably scale performance improvement across a sales team, regardless of experience, competition, or economic conditions. Ultimately, it ensures no sale is lost for the same reason twice.

While it is possible to invest thousands of dollars into a continuous improvement database, it is also possible to do it for free. My own company – along with many of our clients – has been making use of Google Sheets for almost a decade for this purpose. As you prepare to stand up your own Lessons Learned program for your sales team and incorporate it into your weekly sales huddles, ensure your database meets the following criteria:

Shareable Between Team Members

It is imperative that your Lessons Learned database is accessible for each member of your team, and that means it needs to live online. Salespeople need to be able to access the database from home, on the road, in a prospect's lobby, and of course at the home office.

Sortable and Searchable

The Lessons Learned program makes use of pre-defined columns, which allows for ease of input and means that terms can be searched and quickly found by salespeople in the future.

Regularly Revisited

In our clients' companies, the Lessons Learned program is an active part of sales huddles and thus becomes an active part of the lives of salespeople. Not merely a record of what was discussed at a previous sales huddle, a Lessons Learned database also serves as a living record of what salespeople are learning as they adapt and pivot in the ever-changing environment of sales. Standing up a Lessons Learned database for any size team can be done in as little as two minutes and only requires an internet connection, but having a Lessons Learned program languish from misuse can occur in seconds. For this reason, it's imperative that sales managers use it themselves and hold their people accountable for entering data and meeting its accountabilities.

Because Lessons Learned may be a foreign concept, let's walk through a Lessons Learned example so you'll understand how the system works. Then we'll apply it to taking lessons our salespeople bring back from prospecting, outreach, and sales meetings for the benefit of the entire company.

First, State the Situation
(As stated by the salesperson)

Bob, a new salesperson, worked for weeks to schedule a meeting with the executive director of the Widget Manufacturers. Forty minutes into the presentation, Bob discovered that the person he was meeting with would need to consult their CFO and board of directors before investing in Bob's service line. Bob left the meeting with the promise of a follow-up meeting when all parties could be gathered.

Second, What Was the Lesson Learned?

We need to ensure we ask in our discovery calls if the person we're speaking to will need to involve anyone else in the decision-making process. We also need to ensure those additional parties are available to be at the sales meeting before we invest time and money in sending salespeople to a prospect's site.

Third, Who's Responsible for Making the Change?
(What single person in the sales organization is owning the system creation or update that results from what we learned here?)

Charles, the sales manager

Fourth, When Will This Change Take Effect?
(As agreed to by the person owning the change)

October 1, 2021

Fifth, What's Changing?

To justify a meeting with a prospect, especially on-site, salespeople must confirm in account notes that they have asked about the decision-making process to ensure all required parties are present at scheduled sales meetings.

The above scenario may seem like a simple problem that every salesperson encounters at some point in their careers. As a result, many sales leaders treat this as a lesson that each salesperson must learn on their own and hopefully remember. What this tells us is that salespeople are having to *re-learn* the same lessons their predecessors figured out through delayed or lost sales. The result of this is an untold amount of lost revenue.

I understand that if I'm asking business leaders to pull their team out of the field once a week and away from prospect-facing activity to stop forcing salespeople to learn lessons the hard way, I'd better be able to justify it with potential sales and performance growth. I'd been using Lessons Learned in my own company for more than half a decade and seen the results it generated in recaptured time and revenue but needed to express it in a way other sales leader could understand as well.

To make this math simple, let's assume every lesson our team brings back that we implement across our pipeline, campaigns, templates, and/or sales conversations gets them 1% better, and you or your salespeople capture 5 lessons, challenges, or ways to improve your sales systems *this* week. Those 5 lessons create improvements in how you sell that are shared and implemented across your sales team. That represents a 5% improvement in performance across all the salespeople you manage or in your own sales, beginning this week.

Next week, 5 more lessons are captured, and their changes are implemented across your team's systems. Instead of being just 5% better than when you started, in two weeks you're now 10% better (two weeks of a 5% weekly improvement). As you and your team increase performance each week in measurable, trackable ways with your Lessons Learned program, you not only reap the rewards of *this week's* improvements, but also the gains of previous weeks' lessons.

Let's run that compounding performance improvement for a year and see where it takes us:

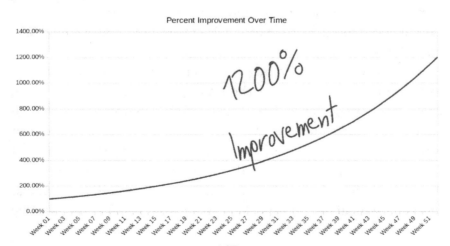

Percent Improvement Over Time

As we can see in the previous graph, with a 5% performance improvement compounded each week by the previous weeks' gains, at the end of the year we see more than a *1200% performance improvement* from where we started.

A few things are worth noting about the impact of a sustained Lessons Learned program in a sales team. First, improvement is consistent. Each week, problems are addressed, solutions presented, and folks held accountable for implementing changes. This sets a tone on any sales team that everyone's improvement is important. Winston Churchill, a man responsible for selling ideas to an entire nation, is famous for saying, "Success is the ability to go from one failure to another without loss of enthusiasm." Knowing that failures are welcome and that tools will be provided for improvement allows salespeople to remain enthusiastic even when their next sales meeting doesn't generate a sale. Using lost sales as a Lesson Learned means it *can* generate a way to improve their chances with the next prospect.

Second, these improvements go beyond the salespeople that discover them. They're built into campaigns, scripts, systems, and onboarding training for the entire sales department, no matter how geographically separated they may be.

Third, it closes the loop on recurring sales challenges. If someone on the team struggles with an issue solved by a Lesson Learned update again, sales managers will have a clear path for retraining.

Fourth, the compounding effect of a 5% improvement each week really kicks in during the final quarter of the year – more than 1/3 of performance gains occur there. While you'll experience freed-up time and increased performance in the first 6 months of rolling out a Lessons Learned program, the second six months will speed you ahead of competition. With major and recurring challenges knocked out, Q4 will be almost entirely dedicated to innovating while competitors will still be putting out fires on their team that you extinguished months ago.

The Lessons Learned program is the engine of a Bulletproof team, whether on the battlefield or in sales, because it is a living document that handles systemic issues that prevent most teams from having the bandwidth to innovate. It's the formula for weaning a team from relying on hope as their strategy.

Because Lessons Learned can generate changes to email templates, call scripts, briefing templates, debriefing checklists, or administrative processes, they're easily updated for every salesperson using a shared CRM. While it should be the business of every salesperson to keep themselves up to date on what's working and what isn't in their industry, the Lessons Learned program feeds them the situations they and other members of their team encountered, what was learned from an encounter or exchange, and what the system-wide update will be to ensure success is replicated or a mistake is avoided.

A side benefit of a robust Lessons Learned program is that it provides a way sales managers can standardize performance across an entire sales team by not just tracking compliance with new systems, but giving your team systems they can *comply with*.

Keep in mind that your Lessons Learned program isn't just a complaint-fest of sales meetings that didn't generate sales. These are 'lessons,' not 'post-mortems.' A post-mortem, by definition, is an examination of something that has died. While your Lessons Learned database will be able to capture situations that resulted in lost sales and prevent them from being lost for the same reason in the future, it is also a place for your salespeople to bring their 'lucky breaks' – the innovations that occur during almost every sale. These are times when the salesperson used their intelligence and professional experience to try something that worked in their favor.

As we dive into systemizing this for your team, let's review the basic layout of the Lessons Learned template as we did with our weekly sales huddle agenda. Next, we'll dive into each section so sales managers understand the meaning of each field and how to enter information.

Once we review each portion of the Lesson Learned flow, we'll walk through an example gathered from a sales meeting debrief and use it to create lasting and permanent change for that sales team. Then we'll go over how to systemize it to update outreach methods, improve conversations, and close more sales.

Systemizing Success with Lessons Learned

This is the format of a Lesson Learned, and the same column headers can be found on our online database, as well as that of our clients':

Situation:	What did we learn?	Who's responsible for the update?	When will the update be made?	What's the change we're making?

Column 1: Situation

The situation section comes first because it is often all the information a salesperson knows when they're entering information. This is the 'from the front line' report they've gathered from sales meetings, initial conversations with prospects, or even administrative issues. If you set a minimum number of lessons for each of your salespeople to bring to sales huddle meetings each week, the 'situation' could be as simple as a software problem they struggled to resolve or something that happened with a particular account. Whatever the situation is, this section needs to be clear enough so that if another salesperson or sales manager has nothing to go off of except what's entered in that one field, they'll have a clear idea of what happened, who it happened to, what account it affected, and when the event occurred and was entered.

The biggest challenge with capturing a complete situation for the first entry in a new Lesson Learned is that salespeople and sales managers usually don't enter enough data. With incomplete data, incomplete improvements inevitably result. Here are the basic areas we suggest clients enter in the 'situation' field to ensure everyone has a clear understanding of the lesson, and anyone revisiting the lesson can understand it:

1. Date of entry
2. Prospect account name (if a prospect account was involved)
3. Salesperson involved
4. Date of the situation
5. What happened

As an example, Jim Cooper, one of your salespeople, brings forward an item captured on his sales meeting debrief checklist that states he didn't ask a prospect about other divisions in their company that could also purchase your product or service. Out of that would come the following entry in the 'Situation' field of your Lessons Learned capture:

Entry: 9/24/2021. Widget Manufacturer's Account, Bob Smith, CEO. Salesperson: Jim Cooper. On 9/20/2021, Jim conducted a sales call via phone, qualified Bob as a buyer, and issued a proposal for one of their divisions. Jim realized after the call that he forgot to ask about any other divisions in Bob's company that could use our service so only priced the proposal for one division. Bob's company definitely meets the size and revenue requirements for follow-on business.

A general rule of thumb in determining how much detail to include in this field is: "If all I had to go off of was what appeared in the 'situation' section, do I have enough information to present a solution that could close the loop on this problem for all my salespeople?"

Column 2: What did we learn?

Basically, this column's entry is the answer to the question:

"If we had to do it over again, what would we do differently with this and all future accounts we encounter this problem in?"

In the case of our example scenario, the entry in this column may look like:

When speaking with a decision maker who manages multiple divisions, we need to ask about additional opportunities before we end a sales meeting or issue a proposal.

Column 3: Who's responsible for making the change?

One of the most important aspects to Lessons Learned entries is they are all assigned a 'Single Point of Accountability' or SPA. Some organizations capture their problems but fewer than 1% go so far as to assign accountability for each problem to single individuals.

In the case of our scenario, this column's entry could be as simple as:

Sally Ross, Training Manager

But why a 'single point of accountability,' when Sally may have a dozen people across other departments that are responsible for implementing this change for her salespeople?

Sales managers and business leaders don't have time to track down a dozen different people to follow up with. That's why it's imperative that no more than one name appears as the single point of accountability on each Lessons Learned entry. A lot is riding on the name entered in this cell, as they're the person responsible for ensuring whatever change that leadership or the sales team decides upon becomes a change that eliminates or mitigates that problem in the future. The benefit to a sales manager, of course, is that they only have to query one individual if they need to check on any aspect of the change this lesson creates.

Column 4: When will the update be made?

If we only take a lesson as far as stating a problem, its details, what we learned, and who's responsible for changing something, we'll have done more than most sales teams – and even most organizations – but I can guarantee whatever action is decided will have a small chance of going into effect without a deadline. While this entry is as simple as a calendar date, it also provides a timeline for whichever SPA owns the lesson to create change.

In the hundreds of times I saw this system used to save lives on battlefields, simply capturing a lesson only benefitted the team involved. If we are creating a Bulletproof sales organization, then we want to ensure that whatever team A learns can also benefit the sales systems of teams B, C, and D. That doesn't happen without a timeline. We'll go over exactly how to take what's on a Lessons Learned sheet and make changes to the Bulletproof sales systems it applies to. If we apply a timeline to our sample scenario, this column's entry may look like:

October 1, 2021

Ensure a specific date is in this column. Not 'Q4' or 'October.' Why? People's minds, and especially salespeople's minds, tend to deal with issues as they become urgent and important. If we have a deadline of 'Q4' for something that isn't setting our hair on fire, then the likelihood of that task being completed before December 31 is slim. Salespeople's hair will always be on fire about something, usually because they're the ones holding the matchbook!

For this reason, list a specific date. If an SPA discovers an update will take longer than the original deadline, the date can always be pushed forward on that entry in the Lessons Learned database.

This leads us to the final column in each Lesson Learned Entry:

Column 5: What's the change we're making?

This is where we ask: "What do we do about it?"

Many sales teams fall flat in creating lasting change at this point. The challenge is not that change doesn't occur, it's that the change is temporary or only stays with the team that discovered it! This is the definition of using hope as a sales strategy, and after all you've learned thus far, hope shouldn't be your first option.

In the case of our scenario with Jim who forgot to ask about other divisions that might need your product or service, this final cell's Lessons Learned entry might look like:

Update the sales script to include questions about other opportunities within the organization for our product or service. Update the sales call debrief checklist to include an item about 'Did we ask about other divisions or areas in this company that could also use our product or service?'

If we express the flow of this particular lesson as it appears on one row in your Lessons Learned database, this chain would unfold:

➢ Situation:
   9/24/2021. Widget Manufacturer's Account, Bob Smith, CEO. Salesperson: Jim Cooper, territory 3 salesperson.
   On 9/20/2021, Jim conducted a sales call via phone, qualified Bob as a buyer, and issued a proposal for one of their divisions. Realized after the call that he forgot to ask about any other divisions in Bob's company that could use our service so was only able to price the proposal for one division. Bob's company definitely meets the size and revenue requirements that would mean they have need for us outside of just the one division.

➢ What did we learn?
   When speaking with a decision maker who sits over multiple divisions, we need to ask about additional opportunity before we end a sales meeting or issue a proposal.

➢ Who's responsible for making the change?
   Sally Ross, Training Manager

➢ When will the update be made?
   October 1, 2021

➢ <u>What's the change we're making?</u>
Update the sales script to include questions about other opportunities within the organization for our product or service. Update the sales call debrief checklist to include an item about 'Did we ask about other divisions or areas in this company that could also use our product or service?'

Now we can see that a single lost opportunity by one of our salespeople generated the lesson that we should be inquiring about additional opportunities in discovery questions across accounts and in all sales meetings. Sally Ross, who oversees training for the sales team will update sales scripts and debrief checklists and is responsible for completing the update by October 1, 2021.

If this was *your* team running this Lesson Learned, understand what just happened:

- One of your salespeople admitted to not doing as well as they could have and was willing to bring it to the group because they're required to bring a certain number of lessons each week to the sales huddle *and* because you have a continuous improvement culture where lessons are welcome.
- Your sales team brainstormed ways to ensure that everyone inquired about additional opportunities across accounts during sales calls, incorporating input from senior and junior team members on the best ways to do it.
- A single person has accountability for updating a system by a specific date.
- A change was proposed that will update across every salesperson's discovery questions and sales meeting debrief checklists to ensure they don't miss inquiring about additional opportunities across every account.

If your salespeople *use* the updated system, which has more to do with their ability to use the systems you've established than *hoping* they'll remember something said at a meeting, what amount of revenue could they recapture? Imagine what it would mean to you as a sales manager to <u>know</u> that each of your salespeople was ensuring they asked about additional opportunities within each of their accounts?

Now imagine walking through at least 5 of these types of updates each week with your team that solved recurring issues that may have existed for decades?

As we've expressed in the performance improvement graph, the accumulated performance gain from Lessons Learned is staggering over the course of a year. Keep it going longer than that, and your sales team won't have competition in their market.

Ensure You Don't Just Address Problems

The value of a Lessons Learned system goes far beyond simply fixing problems or shoring up gaps in your salespeople's skills. It can also be used to amplify and systemize successes. It's tough for a performance-driven sales team to pause after wins and systemize their success. It's even tougher for a sales manager to hold their team back from happy hour after a massive win to do so. But it's just as necessary to capture Lessons Learned from successes as it is from mistakes.

One of the more famous Bulletproof teams I was able to study in the military didn't do their work on battlefields, but rather football fields, parade grounds, and in parks. They're the Silent Drill team, and they're what every marching band, color guard, and baton twirler around the world uses as their standard to measure excellence. What most folks don't know when watching these Marines spin their rifles in perfect timing is that they are witnessing a Lessons Learned program in action.

To watch these Marines is akin to watching a well-choreographed dance. It's hard to believe a few dozen humans can operate in so coordinated a fashion. Harder to believe is that none of the Marines on the Silent Drill Team have been spinning those rifles for longer than 2 years. After a twenty-four-month assignment with the team, each Marine is sent back to the Fleet Marine Force.

I asked their platoon commander how this team was able to conduct flawless performances again and again. He chuckled a bit and said, "Shawn, the Silent Drill Team has been performing for over 70 years, and in all that time, we've never had a perfect performance."

That statement changed the way I viewed my own standard of excellence, and it's changed the way thousands of businesspeople look at their own systems across the clients we've shared it with.

Think back to your last celebration-worthy sale. Maybe it was worth celebrating because of the size of the deal, repute of the client, or the complicated negotiations required. Those are the types of successes salespeople strive to emulate across their careers, but what if such successes were merely the baseline everyone on the team strived for?

What if everything in a sale went right: great pre-call research, identifying and engaging the decision maker with discovery questions, excellent matching of value to desired future state, and the prospect bought the most expensive option? Most salespeople chalk those successes up to their own skill and brilliance. But what if you and your team, as part of your Lessons Learned system, still took the time to ask:

Why did that sale work out so well? If we were going to replicate it, how could we make it even better? How do we systemize those things into every sale from this day forward?

There are lessons that can be drawn out of every successful sale that will benefit your entire team in their future sales. Successes should be solicited from team members along with challenges.

Scaling Lessons Learned on a Large Team

Many sales managers see the value of a Lessons Learned program but are daunted by the prospect of soliciting and managing new lessons each week across hundreds of salespeople. While the next few paragraphs may only apply to those leading larger teams, they're valuable for any sales professional to review because we *should* be building towards having large sales teams. Without Bulletproof systems, it's tough enough to wrangle a few cowboys and cowgirls into individual meetings, let alone sales huddles with teammates. However, systems allow scale. Here's how to do that across a large team with your Lessons Learned program.

While anyone who works more than a few hours a week in a sales position can easily come up with 5 challenges or successes, if we have 50 salespeople regularly reporting 5 new Lessons Learned each week, we now have 250 lessons being submitted every seven days. Some of those lessons will be repeated across teams and some will occur because a salesperson wasn't following an existing system. A few lessons, however, will be innovative or relevant enough to warrant consideration as permanent updates to your organization's Bulletproof sales systems.

What I advise clients overseeing large teams to do is scale their Lessons Learned. While a sales manager can continue to coach individual team members and gather successes and challenges, they can also benefit the entire organization by choosing one lesson from each team's sales huddle that, if codified across all teams, would make a massive difference. Instead of dealing with 250 lessons each week, mid-level leaders now have 50. A regional sales manager, for instance, could then eliminate duplicates among the 50 lessons submitted and share selected lessons with fellow regional managers and vote on which would be the most impactful if implemented across the company. At that point, we've scaled the top 5 lessons each week – culled from 250 submissions, in this example – and can update our entire organization's Bulletproof systems. You can bet those final ultra-impactful changes will carry a greater performance improvement than 5% for those teams.

With a guaranteed way to improve sales performance of 5% every week with no capital cost to our companies, we'd be negligent in our duties as leaders if we didn't begin this process today. The only cost to bear is the discomfort of change. Surprisingly, when it's tied to more sales and more commissions, change is a cost most salespeople are willing to bear.

Whether you are dealing with challenges or deconstructing success, common questions include, "What do I do with the lessons we come up with? How do I ensure they become part of our standard operating procedure and are actually used by our salespeople?"

The benefits really begin for your salespeople when new lessons are used to update existing sales systems or new systems are created. It is also what allows you and your salespeople to take any ideas, tactics, scripts, or checklists picked up from a podcast, book, or sales trainer and ensure they're consistently used across all prospects.

Incorporating Lessons Learned into actual change is a brave new world on the battlefield of sales, and it's where we're headed next.

CHAPTER 19

Sustaining Bulletproof Sales Systems

KNOWING *WHAT* CHANGES to make from hard-earned lessons, and understanding *where and how* to systemize them, are two separate matters. Many sales leaders and veteran salespeople are carrying around hundreds or thousands of best practices in their heads, learned from decades in sales. Additionally, high performers are constantly consuming new sales training material, courses, books, podcasts, etc. Those can potentially generate dozens of new ideas that could improve sales results on your team. How do we insert a lesson our team discovered into existing systems or stand up an entirely new system to ensure what we learn is consistently used?

Systemizing Bulletproof Change

Trigger: When a Lesson Learned is captured, a single point of accountability is assigned, and a deadline is issued for the system creation or update.

Bulletproof Impact: Capturing a lesson ensures a challenge or innovation is outside the heads of salespeople, and updating or standing up a new system ensures the time spent capturing the challenge or innovation was well spent. This is the process of creating and updating systems to ensure they remain Bulletproof.

This guiding question can be used to determine *what* change needs to be made from any lesson you or your salespeople uncover:

"If I wanted to ensure the challenge we encountered in this Lesson Learned was permanently solved – or if what we learned that aided success happened on *every* sale – what system do we need to update or create?"

Bulletproof selling begins with creating and refining systems for your team through establishing not only a pipeline, but also each vertical's campaign systems, the cadence of outreach within those campaigns, templates for those outreach messages, and sales scripts for both discovery calls and sales conversations. We've spent much of this book in those areas because without basic systems in place, it's impossible to create systematic updates. Once established, the Lessons Learned system serves as a sculptor's chisel, carving away rough edges. This is what makes a Bulletproof system adaptable to changes in the economy, technology, market, and customer buying behavior.

If a lesson uncovers a gap in your systems, then it's an invitation to stand up a new one. It's helpful for sales leaders managing their Lessons Learned program to have a map of their Bulletproof sales system in front of them as they determine where a lesson or new tactic should generate a change or update. If you're at a loss for what system a new lesson should create or where an existing system should be updated, examine where in your Bulletproof selling system it might affect:

Bulletproof Strategy
- Pipeline flow
- Campaigns within the pipeline (below are examples, add or remove for your sales cycle and industry):
  - Not a Fit or Hold for Recycle
  - Could Not Reach or Unresponsive Account
  - Initial Outreach

- o Decision Maker Identified
- o Pre-select or Buying Window and Budget Identified
- o Active Opportunity
- o Won Business
- Outreach cadence of the campaigns across communication methods
- Templates of particular outreach tasks (phone scripts, voicemail scripts, email templates, LinkedIn message templates, and card and letter templates)

Bulletproof Tactics
- Calling strategies and scripts
- Handling objections on the phone
- Scheduling sales meetings
- Handling objections in sales meetings
- Using your Bulletproof Offer
- Generating referrals

Administration and Continuous Improvement
- Weekly sales huddle agenda
- Lessons Learned program
- Sales meeting briefing system
- Post-meeting debrief system
- Commission and compensation of salespeople
- Working with other departments in our company to generate leads, sales, and referrals
- Proposal issuance and accounts receivable handoff

Of course, some of those items may not apply to your sales model, and things unique to your industry should be added. Regardless, if a lesson is generated and no one can point to part of your Bulletproof sales system that's already in place where it may apply, it means there's a gap in your armor. In that case, a new system should be created that will bolt onto or follow another existing Bulletproof system in your sales cycle.

Putting Out Fires by Removing the Matchbook

There's a saying that many leaders spend most of their time running around putting out fires until they realize they have the ability to take the matchbooks away from the folks lighting the blazes. Your Lessons Learned program is a way of permanently solving the large and small problems that take up so much time in a leader's life.

If you or your salespeople bring an account forward during your sales huddle and ask what to do about a problem – whether it occurred in a conversation with the prospect, while executing outreach steps, within the CRM's campaign systems, in how a prospect's information was entered into the CRM, or basically anywhere in the lifecycle of a prospect – it can generate a change that prevents *that* question from ever crossing your desk again. How? Create a Lesson Learned from it.

Just as you would do during the Lessons Learned portion of your weekly sales huddle, ask yourself, "If I wanted to ensure the problem that generated that question never happened again, what systems change or training would I need to create, when would that change need to happen, who would be involved in developing or receiving the training, and how would I roll it out?"

What most sales leaders – and leaders in general – tend to do when one of their teammates brings a problem to them is solve it on the spot or formulate a new solution and send the person out to test it. While that method solves the problem in the moment, it does nothing for the next salesperson who runs into a similar situation.

For that reason, ensure that you are also capturing the recurring problems that cross your desk and build Lessons Learned from them. The benefit is that permanently solving problems frees you up to help your team innovate solutions to the endless supply of new challenges coming your way.

While your competition will be struggling to deal with dozens of repeating issues within their own organization, *you* can be the sales team rapidly adapting to your prospect's needs because you solved those repeating issues long ago.

How does a sales leader ensure their Lessons Learned program doesn't become another flavor-of-the-month that eventually goes unused, but instead becomes a tool that regularly elevates the performance of the entire team?

A weekly review of *the last week's* Lessons Learned ensures this happens, and it's why we include it as an agenda item on weekly sales huddles for both ourselves and our clients. Because the world of sales is one of the most rapidly shifting spaces in business, it's critical that any changes to your systems go into effect as quickly as possible. Spending months standing up a single new system or updating an existing system leaves too much room for a competitor to implement it first, especially competitors also using Bulletproof systems. That is why we advise our clients to never make a change so complicated that it takes more than a week to implement, even if the change is overhauling an entire pipeline flow.

The ideas and changes that come from your Lesson Learned program don't have to be perfect and don't have to be pretty. Those refinements will actually come from your salespeople as they use new systems and find ways to make them better, stronger, and more applicable to their prospects' buying cycle. We'll never be able to refine a system if it's never put into place and tested.

It's that never-ending pursuit of progress that makes teams Bulletproof, no matter what odds they stand against or what changes occur on their battlefield. Ensuring your team leverages those changes to *remain* Bulletproof is the topic of our final chapter.

CHAPTER 20

Bulletproofing For the Future

"It is not the strongest of the species that survive, nor the most intelligent, but the ones most responsive to change." – *Charles Darwin,* The Origin of Species

TO SAY WE were travelling light in 2003 would be an understatement. Committed to achieving the objective of racing from Kuwait to Baghdad as soon as possible, the Marines I was with moved so fast across Iraq we often outpaced our supply lines. It was not uncommon to secure a town and then realize our food, water, and ammunition resupply wouldn't arrive for a few hours.

Of course, our equipment was made for this type of mobility. The High Mobility Multipurpose Wheeled Vehicles, or Humvees, lived up to their name. With wooden rails and benches forming their rear beds and nothing but cloth covering the driver and passenger doors, these vehicles were built for speed. Like a bunch of high schoolers packed into the beds of pickup trucks back home, all the Marines riding in back would jostle around as we sped towards our next objective.

That way of travelling, and that way of fighting, worked in 2003. By the end of my second tour in Iraq one year later, everything about those Humvees changed.

Instead of being tasked with racing through towns and across open desert, Marines were tasked with occupying cities, regularly patrolling the same routes. Our opponents realized the wooden rails and cloth doors wouldn't stand up to bullets, let alone bombs, so they began placing improvised explosive devices (IEDs) along our routes. Ever ready to adapt to a changing battlefield, Marines quickly bolted metal plates to the sides of their vehicles and rearranged the seating in the rear bed by installing a single row so Marines could sit facing out and scan their surroundings as they patrolled.

Seemingly overnight, we were traveling in armored vehicles. Something interesting happened that provided a key insight into how to leverage Bulletproof systems in adapting to change.

Specifically, the IEDs our enemies placed on the roads started getting bigger to keep up with our upgraded armor, easily cutting through the metal sheets we'd bolted onto the Humvees. Marines had to not only up-armor their vehicles with even thicker plates but also had to change the way we traveled to minimize the chances of encountering IEDs. The weight of our vehicles changed with the additional armor, affecting maneuverability. It quickly became apparent that the vehicles we'd relied on for more than a decade were not adapted to our new environment. By 2005, we were using an entirely different type of patrol vehicle that shielded everyone inside with bullet-resistant glass and thicker armor.

While the bombs salespeople deal with are of another variety, they do face landmines that can tank sales. As economic forces, pandemics, supply and distribution channels, and market shifts impact our customers, our way of selling must change to keep up.

Thankfully, we don't have to wait for solutions to appear before we can start addressing the coming changes. Because we're using Bulletproof systems, we can adapt them as our salespeople *begin* to notice changes in their markets and customers, rather than when we are forced to change or lose our jobs.

Being willing to adapt to a changing environment, we'll not only innovate at a more rapid pace than competitors, but also better serve the changing needs of prospects and customers.

How do we ensure we are upgrading our Bulletproof systems as the world around us evolves?

While your Lessons Learned program will give you a valuable source of feedback from salespeople on the front lines, we can also involve our entire organizations in regularly upgrading our Bulletproof systems. From the way our accounts receivable department processes customer payments, to the way our delivery teams schedule and deliver our product or service with our clients, to the ways our customer service department ensures our product or service continues to deliver ROI, to our maintenance and upgrade plans that keep our customers coming back – there is no place in a company where we *can't* become Bulletproof. Sales teams should work with everyone in their companies that directly or indirectly serves clients to ensure clean hand-offs from the Bulletproof systems in one department to another.

And let's not forget one of the most valuable sources of feedback for how we can continue to out-innovate every competitor: our prospects and customers themselves.

If we wait until we receive an annual customer satisfaction survey to do something about a systemic problem in the way we sell, deliver, and service our clients, we're leaving massive gaps in our armor that competitors will be all too happy to exploit. Instead of waiting for a customer complaint, our salespeople and *anyone* in our company who interacts with our prospects or customers can take the time to gather lessons and share what they learn to adapt existing systems or stand up new ones.

Customer complaints and concerns are an *invitation* for our companies to become better at what we do.

Better at how we qualify prospects so we're serving those who need us the most.

Better at how we conduct outreach and enhance the methods our prospects best respond to.

Better at how we cut through the noise to demonstrate how our product or service can help in achieving prospect goals.

Better at how we discover additional needs and opportunities in our prospects' companies.

Better at delivering more value than competitors.

Ultimately, being Bulletproof means thriving in the world of sales and actively leveraging the changes we'll inevitably encounter.

What does sales success look like in the future, when the future and the changes it brings are unknown? It's ensuring that at the end of a sale, both our sales team and customers are measurably better than they were before. It means every customer knows *this* experience with our company is better than any transaction anyone's ever had – because our sales team is actively learning, adjusting, and improving every week.

By doing that, competition will have to *hope* they figure out why folks prefer to do business with your salespeople.

But you'll know the real reason. It's because you stopped using hope as your sales strategy.

Instead, you became *Bulletproof.*

BULLETPROOF RESOURCES

Bulletproof Systems Across the Sales Cycle

BECAUSE SYSTEMIZING SALES may be a new concept for some readers, it's helpful to map a typical sales cycle and show where the Bulletproof systems we've shared fit in. This serves as a guide for explaining how Bulletproof systems work throughout a sales cycle, as well as how they generate updates that keep the systems relevant no matter the changes that occur in our market or customers' industries.

Before Contact Is Made

➤ Pipeline Construction: The verticals of a buyer journey are mapped within a CRM.

➤ Campaign Construction: Each vertical or deal stage has an omni-channel campaign assigned to it, complete with templates for emails, direct mail, and social media messaging. Call and objection scripts established.

➤ Prospect Research: 'Qualified prospects' are defined and input into your CRM and prepared for outreach.

Making Initial Contact and Qualifying Buyers

➤ Outbound contact: Salespeople contact the prospect's organization, identify or confirm decision maker(s), and if the prospect is not able to purchase today but will be purchasing soon, place account into a 'pre-select' hold with a firm follow-up date in the CRM. If able to purchase, move to active opportunity or schedule a sales meeting.

Prior To the Sales Meeting

➢ Sales Meeting Brief Conducted: Salesperson and manager or peer meet to conduct a sales meeting brief, utilizing their sales meeting brief script to ensure everything needed is available and research is completed.

During the Sales Meeting

➢ Discovery questions are asked or confirmed, the Bulletproof Offer is presented, and the deal goes to proposal or the next step or a follow-up appointment is confirmed.

After the Sales Meeting

➢ Post-meeting debrief: Salesperson and manager or peer conduct their post-meeting debrief, utilizing their checklist to ensure all necessary data was gathered. Any Lessons Learned captured.

Weekly Meeting and Systems Updates:

➢ Sales Huddle: Lessons Learned from previous week's sales meetings, account activity, and salespeoples' notes discussed. Systems are updated or new systems are scheduled for creation.

Pre-Sales Meeting Brief Guide

To be used by salespeople or managers in preparing for upcoming sales meetings. Ideally, research and data are conducted as soon as the meeting is set by the salesperson and entered in their CRM so it can be easily referenced and shared with the sales manager or peer just prior to the calendar appointment with a prospect.

Name of players involved:
Who will the salesperson be meeting with?

Product or service line to be discussed:
Based on past conversations, which types of products or services offered will this prospect most likely benefit from?

Date and location of service and delivery (if applicable):
If the prospect has date-specific needs, have we confirmed calendar availability for delivery, installation, or presentation?

Anticipated Budget:
Based on past conversations with the prospect, what budget range does this account most likely fall within? If no budget is available, consider logging a Lesson Learned on ascertaining budget with discovery questions.

Phone number and location of meeting and who's making contact:
Where, when, and on what platform is the meeting supposed to occur? Who is calling whom? At what number or what meeting link?

Company details:
What do we know about the prospect company that could be useful in determining product or service line, budget potential, and potential lifetime value? Examples: Number of employees, number of clients, physical locations, prospect's average cost of sale to their customers.

<u>Details about the players involved:</u>
What do we know about the people we'll be meeting with? What does their LinkedIn profile and/or a Google search reveal that could be useful in establishing rapport?

<u>Necessary Materials:</u>
What materials have we committed to bring to this meeting and do we have standard materials ready to present if asked for them?

<u>Possible contingencies:</u>
What contingencies should we be prepared for and have a plan to deal with? Examples: No-show to the meeting, minimum budget does not meet our lowest-tier offering, any tech issues we've experienced recently.

<u>Any questions?:</u>
Final moment for the salesperson to ask any clarifying questions to their manager or peer conducting the brief. If a question arises that should be built into an existing or new system, capture it as a Lesson Learned and update the appropriate system or create a new one.

Sales Meeting Debrief Checklist

To be used immediately after a sales meeting has concluded, conducted ideally by the same manager or peer who conducted the pre-sales meeting brief.

Primary Objective: Did we confirm a decision maker(s), discover their decision-making process, and secure agreement to send the Bulletproof Offer proposal to the buyer with a decision deadline?

Secondary objective: Did we confirm a decision maker(s) and decision-making process with follow-up date to send Bulletproof Offer proposal?

Did we:

_____Confirm whether we're dealing with a sole decision maker or committee?

_____Confirm the decision-making process?

_____Confirm buying timeline?

_____Confirm number of employees or prospect customers our product or service could affect?

_____Discover and confirm objectives for our product or service?

_____Discover or confirm upper limit of budget?

_____Review ability to accept Bulletproof Offer pricing or the need to remove items to meet the budget?

_____Offer additional product lines?

_____Confirm follow-up date and time for next point of outreach?

_____If going to a committee for decision, did we offer to customize a message for them and confirm what date it needed to be delivered by?

_____Is the salesperson connected to the decision maker on LinkedIn?

_____If the decision maker asked for a proposal, who is moving this account into an Active Opportunity?

_____If proposal was requested, which departments will be CC'd?

_____Were referrals requested? Received?

_____Did we capture anything that could be considered a Lesson Learned concerning the salesperson, prospect, or sales manager? If so, what?

Debrief the Salesperson
Guiding Question: "If we knew the answers to the questions we asked during that sales meeting in advance or if we could review a recording of that meeting before it happened, what could we have researched, prepared, or brought with us to be more successful?"

Capture any relevant Lessons Learned that would benefit future sales.

Debrief the Prospect
Guiding question: What did we learn from that sales meeting about that decision maker that would benefit another salesperson if they had to meet with that prospect again?

Capture any relevant Lessons Learned and enter account notes for that prospect in the CRM.

Debrief the Team
Guiding Question: Knowing the questions you'd be asked by the prospect, what could we have provided to you that would have better prepared you for success?

Capture any relevant Lessons Learned.

Weekly Sales Huddle Sample Agenda

This agenda can serve as the backbone of your weekly sales huddles with your salespeople. Refer to the chapter on sales huddles for explanations of individual sections.

Opening:
Set start/stop time of the current meeting

Objectives review:
➤ Review primary sales objective
➤ Review secondary sales objectives

Pipeline Growth:
➤ Team pipeline value growth
➤ Individual pipeline value growth (if review is desired)

Upcoming Opportunity Review
➤ Deals and meetings coming in the next week or month expected to close

Active opportunity reviews
➤ Active proposals out that are expected to close

Individual Account reviews:
➤ Accounts that salespeople have questions about (Capture for Lessons Learned)
➤ Post-Mortem on lost deals (Capture for Lessons Learned)

Continuous Improvement:
➤ Lessons Learned
➤ Record COAs for new systems to handle challenges or innovations discovered
➤ Review last week's LL's that changed or updated systems and ensure deadlines are being met or overdue ones are updated

Accounts receivable review:
➤ (If salespeople need to be kept apprised of accounts receivable funds coming in for commission payouts)

Wins for The Week
➢ Collective or individual wins among the team

Close and Next Meeting Time Confirmed

Bulletproof Selling Lessons Learned Program Reference Guide

The Lessons Learned program comprises of a 5-column spreadsheet:

Situation:	What did we learn?	Who's responsible for the update?	When will the update be made?	What's the change we're making?

Column 1: Situation
In this cell, include:
1. Date of entry
2. Prospect account name (if a prospect account was involved)
3. Salesperson involved
4. Date of the situation
5. What happened

Example: *9/24/2021. Widget Manufacturer's Account, Bob Smith, CEO.*
Salesperson: Jim Cooper.
On 9/20/2021, Jim conducted a sales call via phone, qualified Bob as a buyer, and issued a proposal for one of their divisions. Jim realized after the call that he forgot to ask about any other divisions in Bob's company that could use our service so was only able to price the proposal for one division. Bob's company definitely meets the size and revenue requirements for follow-on business.

Column 2: What did we learn?
This column answers the question:
If we had to do it over again, what would we do differently with this and all future accounts we encounter this problem in?

Example:
When speaking with a decision maker who sits over multiple divisions, we need to ask about additional opportunity before we end a sales meeting or issue a proposal.

Column 3: Who's responsible for making the change?
This column answers the question:

Who's ultimately responsible for making this change?

Example: *Sally Ross, Training Manager*

<u>*Column 4: When will the update be made?*</u>
This column answers the question:
What specific date will this system update or system creation be made?

Example: *October 1, 2021*

<u>*Column 5: What's the change we're making?*</u>
This column answers the question:
What do we do about it?

Example: *Update the sales script to include questions about other opportunities within the organization for our product or service. Update the sales call debrief checklist to include an item about 'Did we ask about other divisions or areas in this company that could also use our product or service?'*

ABOUT THE AUTHOR

Shawn Rhodes leveraged his former life as a war correspondent to become an international expert in how the best teams pivot and scale success. He's a Tampa-based TEDx speaker, and his work studying teams in more than two dozen countries – some of the most dangerous places on the planet – has been published in news outlets including TIME, CNN, NBC, Forbes, the Wall Street Journal, and INC. His clients have included Deloitte, ConAgra, Coca-Cola, and dozens of similar businesses. Shawn is also a nationally syndicated columnist with *The Business Journals* and author of the books *Pivot Point: Turn On A Dime Without Sacrificing Results* and *Universal Export: A Guide For Overachievers in Working Less And Enjoying More.*

Shawn regularly shares the latest sales systems each week through interviews with top sales leaders, the Bulletproof Selling podcast, and articles at www.bulletproof-selling.com.